SCRIPTURAL INSIGHTS AND COMMENTARY

The NEW TESTAMENT

OTHER COVENANT BOOKS AND AUDIO BOOKS
BY TAYLOR HALVERSON:

*Knowing Why: 137 Evidences that the
Book of Mormon Is True*

Millions Shall Know Brother Joseph Again

SCRIPTURAL INSIGHTS AND COMMENTARY

The NEW
TESTAMENT

TAYLOR HALVERSON, PhD

Covenant Communications, Inc.

Cover Image: Jerusalem in her Grandeur, engraved by Charles Mottram (1807-76) 1860 (engraving), Selous, Henry Courtney (1811-90) (after) / Private Collection / The Stapleton Collection / Bridgeman Images

Christ Calling the Apostles James and John, 1869 (oil on canvas), Armitage, Edward (1817-96) / Sheffield Galleries and Museums Trust, UK / Photo © Museums Sheffield / Bridgeman Images

The Exhortation to the Apostles, illustration from 'The Life of Our Lord Jesus Christ' (w/c over graphite on paper), Tissot, James Jacques Joseph (1836-1902) / Brooklyn Museum of Art, New York, USA / Bridgeman Images

Norcia (Italy) © clodio. Courtesy of www.istockphoto.com

Cover design copyright © 2018 by Covenant Communications, Inc.
Cover design by Hannah Bischoff

Published by Covenant Communications, Inc.
American Fork, Utah

Printed in the United States of America
First Printing: October 2018

24 23 22 21 20 19 18   10 9 8 7 6 5 4 3 2 1

ISBN: 978-1-52440-884-8

ACKNOWLEDGMENTS

ANY BOOK IS THE CULMINATION of the efforts and good will of many individuals. I wish to thank those most responsible for making this book a reality.

First, I convey my deep gratitude to Scot and Maurine Proctor of *Meridian Magazine* who believed in my ability to meaningfully explain the scriptures to others and who provided a platform to write and share. They took an unnecessary chance on me, in so many ways, and I, and so many others, have been immeasurably blessed because of their faith, kindness, patience, foresight, and encouragement.

Second, the Interpretation Foundation was generous in providing an additional outlet for my writings in article format. Many thanks to Dan Peterson, Jeff Bradshaw, Brant Gardner, and others who provided volunteer service to review, edit, and format my writing for publication.

I express my appreciation to my friend Kathy Jenkins at Covenant Communications, Inc., who has shepherded this project along into book format and provided important editorial review to improve the flow and readability of the book.

Finally, I thank my wife, Lisa Rampton Halverson, for her ongoing support, her review of all my work with her keen editorial eye, her inspiration and scriptural insights that contributed and informed my writing, and her belief in things that matter.

This work is my own, so my honored friends who have encouraged me should not be held responsible for any errors that may appear.

TABLE OF CONTENTS

SERIES INTRODUCTION

SOME YEARS AGO WHEN I was just fresh off my mission and working a summer job, I took to reading scholarship about the scriptures during my lunch breaks. The readings taught me, built me, and expanded my understanding of scriptures in ways I was surprised to experience, having come off two years of intensive engagement with scripture. My study stirred deep motivations to learn as the scholars had learned about ancient history, peoples, cultures, and places. I wanted to read ancient literature, especially that which would expand my understanding about ancient Israel or the Bible. I felt a swelling desire to master the biblical languages of Hebrew and Greek. The book that set me on this journey was *Isaiah and the Prophets: Inspired Voices from the Old Testament* (1984), edited by Monte Nyman and Charles Tate, specifically the article in that book by Kent Jackson, "The Marriage of Hosea and Jehovah's Covenant with Israel." (I found the book on my mom's bookshelf after I returned from my mission. She had received it as a gift from the CES coordinator in our area of Minnesota to say thank you for her many years of dedicated service teaching early-morning seminary). Little did I realize at the time when I felt so deeply driven to learn how those motivations would be eventually, paradoxically and simultaneously, diametrically deeply fulfilled and frustrated.

I decided to pursue the field of academic biblical scholarship as an undergraduate and graduate student. As I delved deeper into the Bible and the context of scripture, my appreciation for scripture grew in ways I had not anticipated. The beauty and ongoing sustaining power of scripture stunned me. These sacred texts had survived the test of time. These texts have been subjected to nearly ever test and challenge humans could devise, and yet millions of us continue to find them endlessly useful and applicable in our lives. I came to love the scriptures more fully because I understood them more fully. As I knew better, my love and appreciation grew for these texts as it also grew for those who composed and transmitted these documents.

During all this time, my desire to share insights and perspectives with others expanded. I felt a burning desire to help the scriptures be more accessible, applicable, delightful, and engaging. I attempted to fulfill that desire by writing for others what I had found, sharing the excitement of discovering and explaining the meaning and significance.

Strangely, however, the very field that equipped me with tools, knowledge, perspective, and insight about the scriptures to bless the lives of others required that I use my growing content expertise to gain more expertise and then share that only with other content experts, not with regular people. I realized that no amount of content expertise with the scriptures and scripture scholarship would ever be a benefit to anyone else if I couldn't also share with those around me.

So I set to writing.

Over several years I wrote a number of articles on select passages of the standard works of scriptures: the Old and New Testaments, Book of Mormon, Doctrine and Covenants, and Pearl of Great Price. Some of these articles have been published in scattered locations. Now I bring together many of my scripture writings, published and unpublished, into a four-volume set.

My writings are not meant to be exhaustive. I share these articles as samples, hopefully delicious morsels of what a deeper study of select scripture passages can bring to one's soul. My hope is that as readers see how I read (in other words, interpret) scripture, they gain new insights about their own scripture study.

My writing is informed by scholarship, but I am not writing to please a scholarly audience. I hope that scholars find something useful here. But my main intent is that all people will be delighted to dig deeper into the scriptures because of something I have written.

My hope is that these articles are informative, delightful, and engaging to readers. My hope is that readers will return to the scriptures with fresh energy to seek anew. I hope that as readers return to the scriptures, they will find renewal, refreshment, and answers to questions personal and mundane. And most importantly, I hope that my readers will feel the delight one can experience by studying scholarship and scriptures hand-in-hand.

Enjoy the read.

BOOK INTRODUCTION

THIS BOOK GATHERS MANY OF the articles I've composed about the New Testament and the Intertestamental time period (the time between Malachi in the Old Testament and Matthew in the New Testament).

I created this book to share my love of scriptures and scripture study with others. I care deeply about scriptural literacy. Our world is riddled with problems, strife, and conflict. I can't imagine a scenario where improved scriptural literacy could not contribute to more understanding, more empathy, a broader perspective, more patience, and, ultimately, a greater witness for the treasure of truth that is the scriptures.

My hope is that readers will find greater satisfaction in and engagement with scriptures because of the few words that I share here. If my book can stir even one soul to greater dedication to studying the scriptures, as I was inspired by such a book soon after my mission, I would feel that this book is worthwhile. If nothing else, I've felt a sense of fulfilment writing these things hoping that another soul might benefit.

I hope you enjoy the experience.

BETWEEN THE TESTAMENTS:
AN INVITATION TO EXPLORE THE
INTERTESTAMENTAL TIME PERIOD

INTRODUCTION

HAVE YOU EVER TURNED THE Bible page from the last words of Malachi to the first utterances of Matthew? Go ahead. Turn that one page. What do you see? Exactly. Nothing.

Was the world silent between Malachi and Matthew? Absolutely not. But just how much time had passed between the two Testaments? What happened in the eastern Mediterranean world during that time? Did anything happen at all? Could ideas, beliefs, and practices significantly change between the Testaments?

Consider the following: Would we feel historically, ideologically, and politically disoriented if our knowledge of Western history stopped in the year 1492, skipped five hundred years, and then resumed again in the year 1992? Such a thought is absurd. No one could have a complete understanding of the modern world that we live in by skipping such a vast stretch of time during which such enormous changes have occurred in so many aspects of life.

Yet, that is exactly what happens when we turn from the last page of Malachi to the first page of Matthew. Some five hundred years span the distance between these two biblical writers, but we seem not to worry that the political, religious, and ideological worlds that these two writers came from were in many ways radically different from each other. In fact, when we comprehend the flux of change in the eastern Mediterranean world over the course of five hundred years, our newly enlarged understanding of the New Testament will be as wide as the chasm that now marks the apparent emptiness between the Testaments.[1]

---

[1] There are many excellent resources on this time period. An accessible introduction was created by BYU scholars S. Kent Brown and Richard Neitzel Holzapfel in *The*

Unfortunately, we cannot explore here every relevant detail that may enhance our understanding of the New Testament world. Rather, we will focus on some of the key features of change between the Testaments and talk briefly of how knowledge of these changes can enhance our understanding of the New Testament world. Some attention will be given to emerging Jewish groups in the post-exilic world, to ideological changes born in those years, as well as to some of the literature produced between the Testaments. We will also look at the chronological flow of history between the post-exilic times to the New Testament world. With this latter approach, we seek to look at the world of the New Testament not from hundreds of years after the fact, but hundreds of years *before* it emerged. Similarly, with regard to the New Testament itself, it is much more realistic to start many hundreds of years before its composition and look ahead to it through the natural flow of chronology instead of looking over our backs from our own day through successive layers of interpretation that change the color of the original composition.

JEWS RETURN FROM EXILE

As we know, the Jews were led into Babylonian captivity by Nebuchadnezzar around 587 BC. Decades later when the Persians conquered Babylon around 539 BC, Cyrus decreed that the Jerusalem temple should be rebuilt. Some Jews did return to the homeland of Judea, but most stayed in the prosperous circumstances of Mesopotamian cities, including Babylon. Perhaps those that returned from Babylon to Jerusalem were the more religiously zealous, but within a short time spiritual leaders such as Nehemiah and Ezra the Scribe had need to call the Jerusalemite Jews to repentance, for they had forsaken the covenants of the Lord. Later still, Malachi called the priestly class to repentance for focusing more on the rituals of the temple cult than on practicing principles of mercy and justice.

THE RISE OF CANON CONSCIOUSNESS

Ezra's method of calling the Jews to repentance (by means of an appeal to authoritative writings) is representative of one of the

---

Lost 500 Years: What Happened Between the Old and New Testaments (Salt Lake City, UT: Deseret Book, 2006). This 2006 book is the illustrated special edition of their prior publication in 2002 on the same topic: S. Kent Brown and Richard Neitzel Holzapfel, *Between the Testaments: From Malachi to Matthew* (Salt Lake City, UT: Deseret Book, 2002).

key ways that the ideological landscape of Israel changed from Old Testament times to New Testament times. As the years progressed after the Babylonian exile, the Jews gained greater "canon consciousness." To determine what we mean by this phrase, let's briefly discuss what the Bible is.

The word *Bible* comes from the Greek *ta biblia*, which simply means "the books." The Old Testament is just that: a collection of thirty-nine individual books composed by various authors for assorted purposes across many different locales and time periods. The individual books that now comprise our present-day Old Testament were not originally written with the purpose of being included in the Old Testament; the Old Testament did not exist, as we know it, when the individual books were being created. Rather, later groups of Israelites were the ones who recognized the significance of these various writings. They sought to preserve them by copying them, memorizing and reciting them, and teaching them in the synagogues.

It was also of great importance to the preservation process of these religious writings that various groups of Israelites established criteria by which writings could be judged to be of spiritual worth and thus included in the body of literature that spelled out both religious practice and belief.

As a side note, not all groups of Israelites agreed on which books should be included in the authoritative canon. In fact, some of the works that now constitute the Apocrypha and the Pseudepigrapha emerged in this canonization process. Those books reflect the cultural and religious battles taking place between various groups of Jews as they sought to develop a standard canon for belief and practice, which sometimes required exploration of their own beliefs and religious systems. When we understand the world in which the Apocrypha and Pseudepigrapha were produced and the purposes for such literature, we begin to have a deeper understanding of Jews during the Intertestamental time period rather than fearing this so-called "mysterious" literature or misusing this literature as "evidence" for Mormonism.

The canonization process likely began for some Old Testament books before the Babylonian captivity (587 BC), but the process was heightened during and after the captivity for two reasons. First, there was the rise of the scribal class. The scribes spent their lives collecting religious writings, establishing criteria for literature to be included in the canon, and disseminating the doctrines of the standard texts that were allowed into the canon. Ezra was fully part of this scribal class. His knowledge of sacred writings helped to put wayward post-exilic Jerusalem Jews back on track. Second, the Babylonian captivity had been so devastating for the Jewish people that they spent many hundreds of years afterwards doing all in their power to avoid a repeated catastrophe. Many Jews believed that this required closer attention to the laws and rituals of Judaism. But to know these things meant that a common body of sacred writings must be gathered and then shared with all.

Over the course of several hundred years, these processes brought about a uniform and standard canon of authoritative writings for the Jews. As the scribal class disseminated the teachings found in these writings, the Jews in general became more conscious of a "biblical canon"—their set of authoritative writings that defined the boundaries of their belief and practice. Many came to believe that if they adhered to these authoritative writings, they would avoid the disastrous circumstances of exile, foreign invasion, and the wrath of an offended God, though Greek and later Roman dominance challenged these fundamental assumptions.

Thus, the *final* version of the Bible was a product of later Jews (and in some instances Christians), often hundreds of years after the biblical times in which the writings were composed or to which they referred. It is also helpful to note that just as our present-day Book of Mormon was never a complete set of authoritative writings for the people who produced it, so too the Bible was not available, as we know it today, for those who produced the individual works that comprise this collection of "books." Book of Mormon references to writings by Zenos and Zenock suggest that the "canon" of Old Testament writings was not yet set when Lehi and his family left Jerusalem in 600 BC.

Perhaps it is technically incorrect to say that there is a "final version" of the Bible. Every new translation of the Bible is essentially a "new version" that reflects the attitudes, values, and ideals of the time period in which it was translated. This is an inescapable fact. For example, the King James Version (KJV) is reflective of seventeenth-century English culture. How? This is most strongly reflected in the language and grammar used in the translation itself—though this is a somewhat circular reasoning, for what other options did the translators have than to render the original

Hebrew and Greek texts into the common tongue of their place and time? But that is exactly the point. Every time we translate the Bible we cannot help but place our own fingerprints on the work. That does not necessarily mean that we have smudged the Bible or corrupted it; we should have no fear of translating and transmitting the Bible so that it continues to inform our spiritual lives today.

In most cases today, new translations depend on the most ancient and authentic sources (usually Hebrew, Greek, and Aramaic) and not the translations of our own times. In other words, if I was attempting to translate the Bible into Spanish, I would not use the English KJV to do so. Such an approach would preserve the "fingerprints" of the King James translators into the Spanish version as well as adding the new "fingerprints" of Spanish culture and values embedded in the language of the translation. Instead, it would be best to go back to the original languages of Hebrew, Greek, and Aramaic and make a fresh translation from those documents into Spanish. That way the intervening "fingerprints" of the KJV translators would not be preserved and transmitted. This is not to slight the KJV translators. What we are simply attempting to do is to get back to the most original and authentic versions of the biblical text; each translation and each transmission takes us one step farther from the original and pure source.

As later generations of Jews in the Intertestamental period were raised to be aware of an authoritative canon of Jewish religious writings, their world view was very much shaped by the doctrines, beliefs, and expectations they found in the Old Testament. The writers from the Jewish sect called Christianity were well versed in the Old Testament canon. They often and freely quoted or referred to it as they composed their Gospels and Epistles to show how the mission of Christ was a fulfillment of words of prophets written, collected, and preserved over the course of many centuries.

ALEXANDER THE GREAT AND HELLENISM

Now that we have discussed one example of how Jewish world views changed from within, let's return to the history of the eastern Mediterranean and discuss a few ways that outside influences changed the Jewish world. We begin by returning to 530 BC.

After toppling the mighty Babylonians, the Persian Empire persisted for nearly two hundred years, ever seeking to increase its domain and influence. But over time it became a large, inefficient, and proud nation, believing that it was invulnerable to decay or collapse. However, an otherwise insignificant young man from an obscure nation soon radically changed the course of the world forever. He was Alexander the Great.

Born to King Philip of Macedon and tutored by the great Aristotle himself, Alexander was laden with ideas of the promise and glory of Greek culture. He envisioned himself enacting the great exploits of the Greek warriors who fought in the Trojan War, memorialized by the ancient writings of Homer, copies of which Alexander carefully stored under his pillow wherever he went. Alexander also dreamed of bringing the world together in a powerful unity of Greek culture.

At the youthful age of twenty (around 332 BC), Alexander—brilliant, daring, and heedless—amassed an army of Greeks to do battle with an old giant, otherwise known as the Persian Empire. In comparison to the Persians, the Greeks seemed as small and as insignificant in its time as Andorra is to the United States today. The Persians looked on this call to arms as a joke. Yet within the course of a mere ten years, the entire world from Greece to India and Afghanistan to Egypt was ruled and influenced by Greeks.

Soon the Greek language was imported to each of these areas, and with it came the best of Greek learning, including philosophy, astronomy, music, math, medicine, and literature. Greek religion—complete with the myths, rituals, and beliefs that accrued in Greek society over hundreds of years—now replaced or blended with the national and local gods throughout the new empire. People everywhere began to adopt Greek language, thought, and way of life. The adoption and adaptation of Greek culture is called Hellenization (*Hellene* = Greek).

CENTURIES OF POWER STRUGGLES IN PALESTINE

Not all people readily and entirely adopt such enormous changes to their lives. In the age of Hellenism (from around the third to first centuries BC), many sought to retain the beliefs and practices of their own culture instead of that which was offered by the Greeks. Among those who sought to maintain their own ethnic and religious identity were the Jews, even though their communities were scattered across the vast domains under Greek control. The Old Testament canonization process greatly aided in this endeavor, much as the canonical Book of Mormon has helped to establish a common religious culture for Mormons across the world.

But the Jewish efforts met with difficulties. Some Jews discovered the political and financial advantages of adopting Greek customs, while other Jews reasoned that much of the Greek culture would have a benign influence on their own Jewish beliefs and culture, not entirely unlike the challenge believers of today have as they seek to balance their religious life with ubiquitous popular culture. But such mixing created controversy and strife, for there were Jews who felt that the barbaric influences of Greek expansion and culture compromised the purity of Jewish life and doctrine, much like some non-American nations view the negative influence that American Hollywood has had on their own societies. The Apocrypha and Pseudepigrapha preserve some of these religious and cultural controversies of the Intertestamental time period, as did the creative expressions of Greek-cultured Jews exploring their religious heritage with the intellectual tools of Greek invention.

Many Jews at this time were deeply influenced by the intellectual and literary achievements of the Greeks. The Egyptian city of Alexandria (which was home to the one of the greatest universities and libraries of the ancient world) became one of the main centers for Jews to explore how Greek approaches to biblical literature, ideas, and motifs could enhance their understanding of their own Jewish religious and cultural identity. For example, there lived in Alexandria at the time of Christ a man named Philo, a learned Jew who was much enamored with the philosophical doctrines of the Greek philosopher Plato. In Philo's own writings, he essentially rewrote much of the Bible from a Platonic perspective. Years later, prominent early Christians adopted and preserved the writings and ideas of Philo, which influenced the ways in which they interpreted the scriptures for many centuries. In fact, some of those interpretations still exercise authoritative status today.

Other Jews tried to write historical expositions of the Jewish people following the literary examples of Greek historian Herodotus. Still other Jews followed the literary models of theatrical literature (such as the plays of Athenian Aristophanes) and sought to recast famous biblical stories in this new genre, perhaps somewhat akin to what we find today with *Joseph and the Amazing Technicolor Dreamcoat*. These writings, which comprise portions of the Apocrypha and Pseudepigrapha, were not meant to replace the authority of the Bible but rather offer exciting new vistas on an old, yet vibrant faith. What is exciting about these writings is what they tell us about the way Jews between the Testaments understood, interpreted, and lived the Bible. Just as *Joseph and the Amazing Technicolor Dreamcoat* is not an authoritative interpretation of the biblical story of Joseph but rather an expression of how people in our day understand and interpret that story, so much of the Apocryphal and Pseudepigraphic literature of Intertestamental time expresses how Jews understood and interpreted their own scripture. We are free to borrow these latter Jewish interpretations, or we can return to the original biblical texts and find interpretations and meanings that may be more relevant to our current circumstances.

Another reason that conflict arose among the Jews of the ancient Middle East had to do with the political climate imposed on them in the wake of Alexander's triumphs. Alexander died at a young and untimely age. He was but thirty years old (around 323 BC) with the world and her vast treasures at his fingertips when a horrible flu laid him low in the dust to greet death. Alexander's mightiest generals then fought prolonged wars with each other, following the desires of self-interest, to secure their own divided portions of the conquered lands. The state of affairs in Palestine was influenced for more than a century as two of Alexander's generals (Ptolemy and Seleucus) and their descendants warred over this small piece of real estate.

One way that this Greek conflict over Palestine affected the Jewish inhabitants is that those Jews who wanted to rise to power and prominence simply had to exercise some wisdom in choosing political sides to support this ongoing tug-of-war. But such choosing often involved a compromise of Jewish culture and religion to the dismay of those who remained faithful. In fact, some of the Jewish leadership readily adopted Greek customs and ways of life in order to win favor with the Greek rulers.

It is ironic to note, in this regard, that the Jewish position of high priest, the central feature of Jewish spiritual and religious autonomy during the Greek (and later Roman) occupation of Palestine and the epitome of Jewish religious solidarity against the influence of Greek culture, often became a main proponent in introducing Greek culture into Palestine. How did this happen? Often it was Jews from the religio-political camp of the Sadducees (a priestly aristocracy) who vied for the position of high priest. Aspiring Jews paid large sums of money to one Greek political leader or another (Ptolemaic or Seleucid officers, based on which side appeared to be the most powerful at the time) for the position of high priest. The Greek political leader then guaranteed the security of that individual in the position of high priest as long as he was loyal to that particular Greek leader and supported his plan to create a unified culture (in other words, Greek lifestyle) across the kingdom. With such priestcraft going on over the course of many decades, it is no wonder that Jesus so sternly rebuked such treachery.

MACCABEAN REVOLT AND JEWISH INDEPENDENCE

Throughout the long-lasting political and military conflict between the Seleucids and Ptolemaics, Jews found themselves once again as conquered and subjugated people. Though many longingly hoped for the day when independence and Davidic kingship would be restored to them, they learned to live out their lives under less promising political circumstances as long as they were granted the freedom to live according to their ancient beliefs and practices. In most cases, the Greek (and later Roman) leaders recognized the political expediency of granting such religious freedom to the various groups within their empire. What the leaders simply desired was stability, which came through the loyalty (and taxes) of those living within the boundaries of the empire.

Around 175 BC a Seleucid king, Antiochus the IV, came to power and asserted dominion over Palestine. To secure his new-gained political position, he attempted to impose Hellenic culture on all of his people. This was not entirely novel for a Greek ruler; the difference came in what Antiochus IV demanded. After erecting an altar to Zeus Olympus in the sacred precinct of the Jerusalem temple, he commanded the Jews to sacrifice pigs. Some biblical scholars and interpreters see this pagan altar in the temple as the "Abomination of Desolations" referred to in the book of Daniel.

A Jewish priestly family known as the Maccabees, who came from a small town not far from present-day Tel-Aviv, mustered enough influence to stand against the mighty Seleucid army. Within the space of several years (around 165 BC), this family, along with their armies and allies (including a nominal friendship with Rome that soon played into the picture), won Jewish independence, a freedom that the Jews had not known since the Babylonian exile nearly four hundred years earlier. With this new-found political freedom, the Maccabees and their descendants inaugurated one hundred years of Jewish (mis)rule—some of the Maccabean rulers took upon themselves not only kingship, but also appropriated the powers of priesthood, often by paying large sums of money.

THE MANY FACES OF JUDAISM

Not all of the Jews were entirely pleased with the Maccabean religio-political experiment. Various Jewish factions (Sadducee, Pharisee, and Essene) arose that persisted into New Testament times. Biblical scholar John Bright concisely describes each faction and succinctly explains the circumstances in which they emerged:

> With the Maccabean struggle [of 165 BC against the Greeks] serving as a catalyst, Judaism in the second century began to crystallize and to assume the form that it would have in New Testament times. . . . There were, of course, the Sadducees. These drew their strength from the priestly aristocracy and the secular nobility associated with them—the very class that in Seleucid days [prior to 165 BC] had been more than a little tainted with Hellenism. In a certain sense they could claim to be conservatives, for they accorded authority only to the Torah [The Five Books of Moses], and granted none to the body of oral law developed by the scribes. They also rejected such novel notions as belief in resurrection, rewards and punishments after death, demonology and angelology, and apocalyptic speculations generally. It is probable that their foremost concern was that the Temple cult should be prosecuted and the law, especially its ritual and sacrificial features, carried out under the supervision of the constituted priesthood. Whatever they may have thought God's ultimate purpose for Israel to be, their aim in the present was to see to it that this *status quo* was maintained. Being practical men of the world, they were willing to go to considerable lengths of compromise in order to do it, readily cooperating with the secular rulers, whether worldly-minded [Maccabean] priest-kings (who were of their stripe) or Roman procurators, and fearing above all

things any disturbance that might upset the balance—which is why they found Jesus dangerous. For them, in effect, the future of Judaism was to continue as a hierocractic [*hiero* is Greek for "sacred" and often refers to a temple] cult community under the Pentateuchal law [The Pentateuch is a Greek term referring to the Five Books of Moses (Penta = 5)].

Opposite these were, most notably, the Pharisees. These continued the tradition of the Hasidim of Maccabean days, that group whose zeal for the law had allowed no compromise with Hellenism. Though by no means militant nationalists, the Hasidim were driven by the Seleucid persecutions to join in the struggle for religious liberty; but when this was won, and the struggle became one for political independence as well, they tended to lose interest. The Pharisees, who emerged as a party in the course of the second century, were, like the Hasidim, punctilious in their observance of the law. Their relations with the worldly [Maccabean] kings, of whose policies they could scarcely approve, were for the most part strained. Neither an aristocratic nor a priestly clique, their moral earnestness won them widespread respect among the people. Indeed, they became the true spiritual leaders of Judaism and set its tone. Though religiously more strict than the Sadducees, they were in another sense less conservative. They not only accepted other parts of Scripture as authoritative alongside the Torah, they also regarded the oral law developed to interpret the written as fully obligatory. It was through them that this oral law was handed down and expanded, till finally codified in the Mishnah (ca A.D. 200), then in the completed Talmud. The Pharisees quite readily accepted the resurrection. . . . They believed that Judaism's future was to be the holy people of God through keeping the law, written and oral, to the minutest detail; Jews could then await the fulfillment of the promises, which would come in God's own time. Though they . . . [disliked] Roman rule, the Pharisees [avoided] . . . revolutionary activity . . . .

There were, of course, those who felt that the future of Judaism lay along the lines of aggressive nationalism. Men of this opinion had been the backbone of the Maccabean revolt, and the ones who had carried it beyond a mere struggle for religious freedom and turned it into a full-scale war for national independence. The establishment and aggrandizement of the [Maccabean] state under [Jewish priest-king] John Hyrcanus and his successors doubtless satisfied their ambitions and caused militant nationalism for the moment to subside. But the coming of the Roman occupation [ca. 70 BC when the Romans replaced the Greeks, as well as the Jews in Palestine, as rulers of the eastern Mediterranean] which was a galling and humiliating thing to Jewish patriots, fanned the sparks once more to a flame. In New Testament times there had emerged a party of Zealots, fanatically brave and reckless men who were ready to strike for independence against whatever odds, trusting that God would come to their aid. Men such as these precipitated the [Jewish] revolts of A.D. 66-70 and 132-135, which brought the Jewish commonwealth to an end. In their attitude toward the law, Zealots probably differed little from the Pharisees; but they were unwilling to see the future of their nation as one merely of law-keeping—and waiting.

Finally, there were sectarian groups such as the Essenes, who lived in . . . [expectation of the conquering Messiah]. The sect of Qumran, from which have come the Dead Sea scrolls, was almost certainly Essene. . . . Like the Pharisees, the Essenes presumably continued the Hasidic tradition. Their opposition to the [Maccabean] priest-kings was, however, irreconcilable. They . . . regarded the [Maccabean] priesthood as illegitimate and apostate. At some time, probably in the last third of the second century, they withdrew in the face of opposition from Jerusalem and from participation in the Temple cult, and took refuge in the wilderness of Judea, where they pursued a quasi-monastic existence in preparation for the impending end. It was, apparently, among the Essenes that the Jewish apocalyptic tradition was carried forth, and much of its literature produced. They regarded themselves as the people of the New Covenant; they had their own peculiar interpretation of the law, their peculiar religious calendar, and they were pledged to a strict discipline with was rigorously enforced. They awaited the imminent end of history's drama, the outbreak of the final struggle between light and darkness, God and evil—which would also involve a holy war on earth in which they expected to participate. Convinced that all prophecy was being fulfilled in their day, they commented upon various Biblical books to show that this was so. The importance of Essene belief for understanding the background of New Testament thought is a subject to itself.[2]

JEWISH SECTS AND THE NEW TESTAMENT

We are greeted with two of the above-mentioned groups (Sadducees and Pharisees) throughout the pages of the New Testament. They are constantly at odds with Jesus, who continually points out their failure to exhibit true righteousness. Both of these groups believed in their own innate righteousness—the Sadducees because they were the line of priests and held the privilege of officiating in the temple, and the Pharisees because of their zealous observance of Jewish practice found both in the written and oral law. Nothing could be more grating to someone who believes in his own goodness and righteousness than to be called to repentance, by a carpenter no less! (What insignificant Galilean town was He from again?). The Essenes are not mentioned in the New Testament but are of interest to us because of their connection with the Dead Sea Scrolls and the way that those scrolls inform our understanding of Judaism and Christianity at the time of Christ.

LOSS OF JEWISH INDEPENDENCE—ROMAN DOMINATION

Some of the later Maccabean rulers were excessive in their pride and wickedness, even going so far as to subjugate other peoples and forcibly covert them to Judaism. One such subjugated group was the Idumeans, the people of Herod the Great. Around 70 BC, two Jewish brothers (Hyrcanus II and Aristobulus II), heirs and descendants of the Maccabean priest-kings, quarreled for power. One appealed to Rome for intervention; the end result was Roman general Pompey occupying Jerusalem and annexing the region of Palestine as the Roman province of Judah. Thus, Jewish political independence was again forfeited to foreign (read Gentile) rulers.

The more pious of the Jews who felt that an adoption of Greek culture or Roman administrative structure was a transgression against canonized biblical standards longed for the revolutionary days of the Maccabees when the faithful stood united against "gentile" incursions. These tendencies and desires remained tacitly in the Jewish psyche for hundreds of years afterwards. (Consider that there was an open Jewish

---

[2] John Bright, *A History of Israel* (Philadelphia: Westminster Press, 1981), 460–463.

revolt against Rome in 66 AD that resulted in the destruction of the temple. Then in 132 AD, the Jews again revolted against Rome, for which they were dispersed from the province of Judah by imperial edict.)

These events are one of the reasons why some of the Jews were looking for a political Messiah when Jesus arrived one hundred years after Pompey brought Roman rule to Palestine. It was Roman administrative rule and the Greek culture (that had conquered the conquering Romans) that provided the backdrop for the world of the New Testament, a world that had once been dominated by independent Israelites and later by Babylonian and Persian authority.

A SUMMARY

We have raced through nearly five hundred years of history at a speed that would make even Einstein rethink the laws of relativity. However, the purpose was simply to offer a sense for the turbulent world of change. Sometimes we view the ancient past with an idyllic lens through which life seems serene, timeless, and changeless. What we discover, however, is that culture was vibrant, religion was compelling, and politics were just as divisive as they are in our own day. The only difference was in the expression of these different facets of life.

When we look at the ancient past knowing that it was populated by people who lived, loved, and learned, we see similar patterns, even though they are expressed in unique colors and hues. When we look on these ancient expressions in their original colors and hues without imposing on them our own predetermined, preconceived colors and hues, barriers to understanding are broken down, and their life struggles and triumphs suddenly become relevant and useful for our own day. In other words, if we truly hope to understand the people of the ancient past who produced the literature that we call scripture, we must follow the common wisdom of "stepping into their shoes." We must temporarily let go of and replace our own worldview and perspectives with theirs if we ever hope to truly understand them.

AN INVITATION FOR THE ONWARD JOURNEY

One of the best ways to understand the worldview of another is by reading what they have written. While you now have just a brief survey of a few ways the world changed between the Testaments, you have a sufficient foundation for understanding some of the cultural and religious institutions, political conflicts, and moral needs that shaped the New Testament world. More importantly, this historical survey also provides a backdrop for more fully exploring the many literary resources produced by the Jews during the Intertestamental time period that preserve the beliefs and practices of the various Judaisms alive at that time, which can greatly aid us in "stepping into their shoes."

I consciously use the term *Judaisms* to highlight the reality that there was not one single, standard version of Judaism. For example we have Pharisaic Judaism, Hasidic Judaism, Essenic Judaism, Sadducean Judaism, and others. In fact, the existence of so many expressions of Judaism over many centuries is what provided fertile ground for the Jewish sectarian movement now known as Christianity. During the Intertestamental period, most of the fifteen Apocryphal writings and many of the ninety Old Testament Pseudepigraphic writings were written in various locales where Jews resided (such as Palestine, Egypt, and Babylon). These writings often reflect the cultural environment of Hellenization, the ongoing political conflicts of various regions, or the exercise and exploration of Jewish belief and practice. (A great starting point for delving further into these ancient writings is James H. Charlesworth's two-volume set of *Old Testament Pseudepigrapha*.)

I SAW THE HEAVENS OPEN: JOSEPH SMITH'S INSPIRED TRANSLATION OF THE BIBLE

"He saw the heavens open . . . and . . . he saw One descending out of the midst of heaven . . . [who] stood before my father, and gave unto him a book, and bade him that he should read. And it came to pass that as he read, he was filled with the Spirit of the Lord." —1 Nephi 1:8-9, 11-12

WHO AMONG US HAS NOT longed to have the heavens open and the blessings of revelation flow unto us through the Spirit of the Lord? And who among us has not desired to know what Lehi or Nephi or Alma or Joseph Smith knew? Mighty and pure were the truths that they taught and the doctrines they knew—indeed the heavens were opened to them and revelations poured forth like a flood (see Malachi 3:10). What would it require for any one of us to have such an experience? The process begins when we open the scriptures to explore the heaven-revealed words of the prophets.

Of the heavenly treasures bestowed on God's children, one of the greatest is Joseph Smith's inspired translation of the Bible. Herein was the work of scripture being enhanced by a living prophet who had seen into the heavens. Soon after the publication of the Book of Mormon in 1830, the Lord commanded Joseph to begin this monumental work. The Lord promised:

> Behold, I say unto you, it shall not be given unto you to know any further . . . until the [scriptures] be translated, and in it all these things shall be made known. Wherefore I give unto you that ye may now translate it, that ye may be prepared for the things to come. (D&C 45:60–61.)

This inspired translation was mostly complete by 1833. However, the Church members of Joseph's day neglected to support the cause of bringing forth new scripture, which hindered these new scriptures from being published by The Church of Jesus Christ of Latter-day Saints until 1979; even then, *only one-third* of Joseph's inspired revisions were included![3] Even in our day, these powerful scriptural revelations sit quietly tucked away in the back of our Bibles or unnoticed in a plethora of footnotes with a small abbreviation that reads JST. Portions of the Joseph Smith Translation are found in the Appendix of the LDS King James Version Bible

Like the prophets of God, we can begin to have the heavens opened unto us as we more carefully explore and ponder the inspired words of the Joseph Smith Translation (JST). Let's take as one example a passage from Matthew concerning John the Baptist's interaction with the Pharisees and Sadducees as he baptized at the Jordan. We will compare in parallel columns beginning on the next page Joseph Smith's inspired version against the King James Version translation (KJV). This will give us a taste of the marvelous doctrines available to any who will but seek them in these new scriptures.

All of Joseph Smith's inspired revisions are marked in **bold**. Portions of the KJV *not* found in the JST are marked in *italics*.

WHAT DO WE LEARN?

There is much more that the Joseph Smith Translation has to offer than we may have first imagined. Additionally, the bold-highlighted text clearly emphasizes how many changes there truly are between the KJV and the JST. Let's carefully explore some of these textual differences verse by verse.

JST Matthew 3:33

Though this is not of any doctrinal significance, Joseph Smith included an exclamation point (!) after the word *vipers* to highlight the intensity of John the Baptist's rebuke to impenitent Jews.

JST Matthew 3:34

Here we have a pearl of great price! Words of the prophet John the Baptist that were not transmitted across the ages have been revealed anew in our day. His words, which are found only in the Joseph Smith Translation, are truly a profound expression of three key doctrines:

---

[3] Robert J. Matthews, *A Bible! A Bible!* (Salt Lake City: Bookcraft, Inc., 1990), 91.

John the Baptist was the Elias (forerunner) for Jesus Christ, preparing the hearts of the people to receive the greater which was to come.

Those who reject the servants of the Lord (the forerunners who come beforehand proclaiming that the kingdom of God is at hand and that all must repent to enter in) will not accept the Lord Himself when He comes.

The Atonement of Christ cannot cover the sins of those who do not accept Him.

What is so beautiful here about John the Baptist's language is the use of the term *cloak.* The word *cloak* is often used to refer to a "loose outer

JST Matthew 3:33–40*	KJV Matthew 3:7–12
33 But when he saw many of the Pharisees and Sadducees come to his baptism, he said unto them, O, generation of vipers! who hath warned you to flee from the wrath to come? **34 Why is it that ye receive not the preaching of him whom God hath sent? If ye receive not this in your hearts, ye receive not me; and if ye receive not me, ye receive not him of whom I am sent to bear record; and for your sins ye have no cloak.** 35 **Repent**, therefore, **and** bring forth fruits meet for repentance; 36 And think not to say within yourselves, We **are the children of** Abraham, **and we only have power to bring seed unto** our father Abraham; for I say unto you that God is able of these stones to raise up children **into** Abraham.	7 ¶ But when he saw many of the Pharisees and Sadducees come to his baptism, he said unto them, O generation of vipers, who hath warned you to flee from the wrath to come? 8 Bring forth therefore fruits meet for repentance: 9 And think not to say within yourselves, We *have* Abraham *to our* father: for I say unto you, that God is able of these stones to raise up children *unto* Abraham.
The New Testament of Our Lord and Savior Jesus Christ: An Inspired Revision of the Authorized Version by Joseph Smith Junior (Independence, MO: Herald Publishing House, 1991)	

37 And now, also, the axe is laid unto the root of the trees; therefore every tree which bringeth not forth good fruit, **shall be** hewn down, and cast into the fire.

38 I indeed baptize you with water, **upon your** repentance; **and when** he **of whom I bear record** cometh, **who** is mightier than I, whose shoes I am not worthy to bear**, (or whose place I am not able to fill,) as I said, I indeed** baptize you **before he cometh, that when he cometh** he **may** baptize you with the Holy Ghost and fire.

39 **And it is he of whom I shall bear record,** whose fan **shall be** in his hand, and he will **thoroughly** purge his floor, and gather his wheat into the garner; but **in the fullness of his own time** will burn up the chaff with unquenchable fire.

40 **Thus came John, preaching and baptizing in the river of Jordan; bearing record, that he who was coming after him had power to baptize with the Holy Ghost and fire.**

11 I indeed baptize you with water unto repentance: *but* he *that* cometh *after me* is mightier than I, whose shoes I am not worthy to bear: he *shall* baptize you with the Holy Ghost, and *with fire*:

12 Whose fan is in his hand, and he will *throughly* purge his floor, and gather his wheat into the garner; but *he* will burn up the chaff with unquenchable fire.

garment" or "something that conceals."[4] The Atonement of Jesus Christ does just that: it covers us like a cloak or garment of light and conceals all of our sins and iniquities against the justice of God so that we are radiant and pure before the Lord as we enter into His kingdom.

Significantly, the English word *atonement* is translated from the Hebrew word *kefar*, which is etymologically rooted to the English word *cover*, which is similar in meaning to "cloak." Notice the similarity in pronunciation between the Hebrew *kefar* and English *cover*. It is also significant that the emblems of the Atonement are blessed and administered to us each week in dedicated chapels, which spiritually function as cloaks. Not surprisingly we discover that the word *chapel* comes from the Late Latin word *cappa*, which means "cloak."[5]

So what John the Baptist is saying to the Pharisees and Sadducees in a conversation entirely absent in the KJV is that those who reject him will also reject the Savior. And those who reject the Savior will have nowhere to hide, nothing to cover them in the day of judgment as they cry out "to the mountains, Fall on us; and to the hills, Cover us" (Luke 23:30). A similar sentiment is found in 1 Nephi 12:9–10, "And the mean man boweth not down, and the great man humbleth himself not, therefore, forgive him not. O ye wicked ones, enter into the rock, and hide thee in the dust, for the fear of the Lord and the glory of his majesty shall smite thee."

JST Matthew 3:35

In this verse, the inspired version adds "repent" to the beginning of the verse, which makes for a stronger connection between John's statements that the wicked have no covering and their need to call on the Lord for spiritual safety. Without the introductory "repent," the strength of the message is muted, as we find in our current KJV.

JST Matthew 3:36

The inspired changes to these verses are subtle yet profoundly significant. In the JST version, the Pharisees and Sadducees say to themselves that they are the ones who raise up seed to (or on behalf of) Abraham. This statement entirely leaves out of the Abrahamic covenants

---

4 Merriam-Webster Dictionary, 2001. See "cloak."

5 Merriam-Webster Dictionary, 2001. See "chapel."

any who are not of the literal seed of Abraham. Yet John counters that prideful and false notion—that only the literal seed of Abraham are covenant people—by testifying that God can raise up posterity *into* Abraham with stones. The "into" of this verse means "adopted." In other words, John testifies that all of those who accept Christ will be adopted *into* Abraham, *into* the family of Abraham, *into* the Abrahamic covenants, and *into* the kingdom of the Lord. Unfortunately, the Pharisees and Sadducees had trusted in their genealogy instead of the power of repentance and the Atonement of Christ; the kingdom will not be comprised just of those who are of the literal seed, as they erroneously assumed. Thus the JST translation of this verse further reinforces the doctrine of adoption, casting the gospel net to the four corners of the earth instead of simply to those who are of blood lineage.

JST Matthew 3:37

The JST translation simply highlights a tense change and is not of any major doctrinal significance.

JST Matthew 3:38

In this verse, the inspired translation doctrinally clarifies the purpose and sequence of repentance and baptism. The KJV translation makes it appear that an individual is baptized *and then* repents. Instead, as stated correctly in the JST, baptism is the sign of repentance:

> Yea, I say unto you come and fear not, and lay aside every sin, which easily doth beset you, which doth bind you down to destruction, yea, come and go forth, and show unto your God that ye are willing to repent of your sins and enter into a covenant with him to keep his commandments, and witness it unto him this day by going into the waters of baptism. (Alma 7:15)

The JST correctly transmits the doctrine of repentance and baptism in the saying, "I indeed baptize you with water, *upon your repentance.*"

Additionally, in this verse the JST further witnesses of John's preparatory purpose to baptize souls so that they might receive the baptism of fire and of the Holy Ghost from Jesus Christ. The KJV version does not plainly manifest this aspect of John the Baptist's mission.

JST Matthew 3:39

In addition to emphasizing John's mission to bear witness of the Savior, there is one key point that this JST verse captures concerning the wicked. The KJV indicates that the wicked will burn, but the JST indicates a time period,: in the fullness of the Lord's own time.

JST Matthew 3:40

This verse is entirely absent in our current KJV translation of the Bible. How simple, yet how pure and profound in doctrine it is and how well it synthesizes and summarizes the main ideas of all the previous verses.

THE TREASURES OF HEAVEN

How richly blessed we are with the additional scripture received by one who had gazed into the heavens and contemplated the deep things of God. How good God has been to us to bring these things forth in our time. And how much more will be our blessing when we diligently search that which we already have before us, for it is then that we will be prepared to receive more.

> He saw the heavens open . . . and . . . he saw One descending out of the midst of heaven . . . [who] stood before my father, and gave unto him a book, and bade him that he should read. And it came to pass that as he read, he was filled with the Spirit of the Lord. (1 Nephi 1:8–9, 11–12)

May we see into heaven through the eyes of the prophets. And may we be like Lehi, who followed the Lord's command to open the scriptures and read. By availing ourselves of the Joseph Smith Translation and other scriptures, we will be filled with the Spirit of the Lord and proclaim with Lehi: "Great and marvelous are thy works, O Lord God Almighty! Thy throne is high in the heavens, and thy power, and goodness, and mercy are over all the inhabitants of the earth" (1 Nephi 1:14).

MATTHEW 1 AND LUKE 1: TESTIMONIES OF JESUS

AS WE APPROACH OUR STUDY of the scriptures, may we be like the inquisitive Theophilus of Luke, searching for the certain witness of the Lord Jesus Christ (see Luke 1:1–4). To satisfy such spiritual desires, faithful early Christians such as Luke composed lengthy expositions called "Gospels" filled with narratives, homilies, hymnodies, miracles, parables, sayings, doings, doctrines, and, most importantly, the sure witness of Jesus as the promised Christ.

We have four such Gospels in our canonical New Testament that share this testimony of Christ. But just as four master painters use various styles to represent the same landscape, so too the four Gospel writers have unique approaches to sharing their certain witness that Jesus is indeed the Christ. Additionally, each of our Gospel witnesses includes unique perspectives and valuable information as he describes life models of worthy and God-fearing individuals who populate the stage of Christ's life, such as Mary, Joseph, and John the Baptist.

The first chapter of both Matthew and Luke contain unique expressions of Christ-centered testimony.

MATTHEW'S TESTIMONY

Like the other Gospel writers, Matthew approaches his task with a desire to testify of Jesus. His focus, however, has some unique aspects.

First, Matthew delights in testifying that Jesus is the covenant Messiah. Matthew's genealogical account begins with Jesus as a son of David and a son of Abraham. David and Abraham are the most notable for the covenants God made with them, covenants that also apply to their descendants and their people, the Israelites. To Abraham, God covenanted property, posterity, and priesthood (see Genesis 15 and 18), all of which are promises of eternal life guaranteed by Christ to the faithful. To David, God covenanted to establish His throne forever, a covenantal promise fulfilled by David's true heir to the throne, Jesus Christ.

Second, Matthew stresses that Jesus is the covenant Messiah by means of the numbered generations he employs. In some circles of Jewish thought, numbers held symbolic significance. For example, the number 3 represented "covenant" and the number 14 represented "Messiah." In the genealogical list are several individuals who are of the fourteenth generation and thus are a messiah figure. David is one of these. Matthew is careful to note that Jesus is the third of fourteen generations. Not only is Jesus a messiah figure (since He is of the fourteenth generation) but indeed Jesus is *the* covenant Messiah because He is the third fourteenth generation.

Matthew also shows that Jesus is the Jewish Messiah. Again we turn to Matthew's genealogical introduction for evidence of this testimony. Notice that Matthew highlights some of the most honorable and noteworthy individuals of the Israelite/Jewish family. The same two heroes mentioned above, Abraham and David, are the first to begin the list, highlighting Jesus's connection to the greatest Israelite heroes. Other honorable Jews are also found in the list, such as Zerubbabel, builder of the Second Jewish Temple after the Babylonian exile, and Boaz, who married the Moabite Ruth. What is interesting about the inclusion of Ruth is that she was a gentile woman. Matthew also lists the union of Judas and Tamar (a union of infidelity). What does this tell us? Matthew indicates with his genealogy that Jesus truly is the Jewish Messiah but He is also the Messiah for all peoples in whatever circumstance they may be.

Fourth, Matthew testifies of Jesus as the royal Messiah. This again is linked to the covenants of an everlasting throne that God promised to King David. Additionally, a careful reading of Matthew will reveal that Jesus is indeed heir to the throne of David through direct father-to-son lineage.

One final aspect of Matthew's style that we should mention here is his knowledge of the Old Testament and his tendency to draw on those scriptures to establish that Jesus is indeed the promised Messiah of the Old Testament. As you read through the Gospel of Matthew, keep these characteristics in mind and perhaps record the ways that these characteristics are expressed in later chapters.

LUKE'S TESTIMONY

Luke most likely was writing his testimony of Christ for an audience that had not grown up with the Jewish faith. He was careful to portray Jesus as the Messiah of all people, but more than the other Gospel writers Luke focused on the humility of the Savior and His special mission to the meek, lowly, oppressed, and down-trodden. We see in Luke 2 his version of the Christmas story, complete with humble shepherds and a humble birth in a lowly stable. Contrast this to Matthew's Christmas story (in Matthew 2), which focuses on the royal characteristics of Christ's birth (for example, kingly men give Him the gifts normally accorded a king). These two views of the same event richly enhance our understanding of Christ and His attributes.[6]

Another way that Luke testifies of Christ is by appealing to beautiful psalms and hymns expressed by faithful saints such as Mary and Zacharias. In fact, nearly half of the first chapter of Luke is devoted to the psalms sung by Mary and Zacharias (see Luke 1:46–55 and 69–80, respectively). These two New Testament psalms are also called *The Magnificat* (Mary) and *The Nunc Dimittis* (Zacharias).

SAINTS OF NEW TESTAMENT TIMES

In their opening chapters, Matthew and Luke introduce us to several New Testament characters, individuals who stand as models of righteousness: Mary, Joseph, Elizabeth, Zacharias, and John the Baptist.

Mary: The Mother of God

The name *Mary* derives from the Hebrew name *Miriam*, which means "bitter." At first glance, we may consider that the name for the mother of God is inappropriate given the sweet and beautiful role she played in the plan of salvation. Upon a little more reflection, though, we remember that Miriam was the sister of Moses, who likely received the name "bitter" to reflect the awful reality of Israelite bondage to the Egyptians. But it was Miriam who led the women of Israel in praise, song, and mighty rejoicing after the Lord delivered them through the Red Sea. Indeed, Miriam is even called a prophetess in Israel (see Exodus 15:20–21). In this light, Mary the mother of God has a worthy namesake.

---

6 John W. Welch and John F. Hall, *Charting the New Testament* (Provo: Foundation for Ancient Research and Mormon Studies, 2002), chart 7–3.

Joseph—Surrogate Father

The name *Joseph* is of promise to us, for in Hebrew it means "God will increase." This is both a worthy and fitting name for the role that Joseph played for Jesus. Indeed, God did bring increase through Jesus—an increase of love, meekness, righteousness, power, light, truth, and knowledge. We may also find fruitful parallels between Joseph of Egypt and Joseph the carpenter. Both went into Egypt under dire circumstances, and in both situations the sojourn in Egypt proved to be an act of salvation for Israel.

We may know the meaning of the name *Joseph,* but we know precious little of the man named Joseph who was the earthly father of Jesus. Based on Matthew's genealogy, Joseph was heir to the throne of David. Yet from what we can surmise, he spent his days in obscurity and likely poverty as a Nazarene carpenter. We can recognize the integrity and good heart of such a man who, when he discovered that his fiancé was expecting a child, chose to not to shame her or publicly expose her. In fact, he moved forward with his plans to marry her.

Unfortunately, this is about all we know of Joseph. We hear nothing else of Joseph after the young family returns to Palestine from Egypt except for the temple episode when Jesus was a mere lad of twelve years. Perhaps Joseph passed away before Jesus's formal ministry began. We do not know. Though speculation may be interesting, it generally offers few definitive rewards.

Zacharias—Father of John the Baptist

Zacharias is the Greek version of the Hebrew name *Zechariah,* which means "Jehovah remembers." After many years of silence, when no prophet was found in Israel, Jehovah remembered His covenants to the children of Israel. He raised up a new prophet to sound the warning voice.

It is interesting to note that Zacharias's namesake was a prophet of the Old Testament who prophesied of the coming Messiah of Zacharias's own kin. Consider a few of the words of Old Testament Zechariah and then remember how they began to be fulfilled in Zacharias's own day:

"Rejoice greatly, O daughter of Zion; shout, O daughter of Jerusalem: behold, thy King cometh unto thee: he is just, and having salvation; lowly, and riding upon an ass, and upon a colt the foal of an ass" (Zechariah 9:9).

This prophetic statement of Zechariah is like the clarion call of Zacharias's son John for Israel to behold their king and make His paths straight. Also compare the above passage to Jesus's triumphal entry to Jerusalem described in Matthew 21.

Here are additional messianic prophesies from Zechariah and how they relate to the New Testament:

Zechariah	New Testament
"As for thee also, by the blood of thy covenant I have sent forth thy prisoners out of the pit wherein is no water." (Zechariah 9:11)	"For Christ also hath once suffered for sins, the just for the unjust, that he might begin us to God, being put to death in the flesh, but quickened by the Spirit; by which also he went and preached unto the spirits in prison . . . for for this cause was the gospel preached also to them that are dead, that they might be judged according to men in the flesh, but live according to God in the spirit." (1 Peter 3:18–19; 4:6)
"So they weighed for my price thirty pieces of silver." (Zechariah 11:12)	"Then Judas . . . brought again the thirty pieces of silver . . . and he cast the pieces of silver to the chief priests and elders, saying, I have sinned in that I have betrayed the innocent blood." (Matthew 27:3–4)
"What are these wounds in thine hands? Then he shall answer, Those with which I was wounded in the house of my friends." (Zechariah 13:6)	"He shewed unto them his hands and his side. Then were the disciples glad, when they saw the Lord." (John 20:20)

Elisabeth—Mother of Israel's New Prophet

Elisabeth is a beautiful Hebrew name that means "consecrated to God," a name entirely worthy of a woman who consecrated her greatest desire to God—the desire to have a child. In this regard, Elisabeth is in league with many of our most revered matriarchs from the Old Testament, such as Sarah, Rebecca, Rachel, and Hannah, who all struggled with barrenness.

We remember that Hannah covenanted to consecrate her child to the Lord if He would grant her the blessing of bearing a child. The vow that Hannah made to the Lord is called the "Nazarite vow," which includes promises that a razor would never come to the head of the child and that the mother would abstain from strong drink and any unclean thing as she carries the child. Hannah's prayer was answered, and several years later she presented the young boy Samuel to Eli, the high priest over Israel in that day. Samuel later became one of the greatest prophets Israel had known, anointing King David, who in turn inaugurated Israel's "Golden Age."

This episode is similar to another Old Testament story in which a barren woman invoked the Nazarite vow as she pleaded with the Lord to bless her with a son. An angel appeared to the woman with a promise that God would bless her according to her desires. The son she bore, upon whom a razor never was to fall, was the famed and mighty Samson, who delivered Israel out of the hands of its Philistine enemies. (Of course, Samson late broke the covenant, cut his hair, and lost the strength of the Lord, a reminder to all of us to remain true to our covenants.)

Barren Elisabeth is like so many other faithful Old Testament women who heard the voice of angels promising a child of much hope. In Elisabeth's case, her child was one of the greatest prophets ever to raise a voice in Israel.

John the Baptist

Like other mighty men born of promises to barren women, John, whose name means "God is gracious/God is merciful," lived a life much along the lines of a Nazarite vow (such as Samuel and Samson). He lived in the wilderness, feeding off locusts and honey, wearing camel's hair, and being perceived generally as a wild man from the desert. But he came to prepare the way of the Lord and to make His paths straight.

Significantly, John's birth, 180 days before that of Jesus, did symbolize making the pathways straight, for 180 degrees is a straight line. Just as Samuel the prophet prepared the way for David to be king over Israel by anointing him for that end, John the Baptist was a mighty prophet preparing the way for the true king of Israel, baptizing Him for that purpose. And just as Samson was a judge and deliverer of Israel from her enemies, John the Baptist prepared the way for New Testament Israel to be saved from her most pressing enemy, namely Lucifer.

SEARCH THE SCRIPTURES

What was covered here is but a small sampling of the many marvelous treasures packed into the scriptures. These treasures are available to each of us—and finding those treasures simply requires a portion of God's Spirit and the effort on our part to open the scriptures and experience for ourselves the magnificent blessings of God's word. As we carefully read and ponder the scriptures, we discover the amazing richness of individuality of expression among the various writers. Each unique voice offers tantalizing ways for us to ponder the scriptures; each approach can bring a wealth of understanding. When we know the authors as individuals, when we understand nuances and characteristics of each as an author, our scriptural experience can be enhanced. And when we combine these unique voices, a veritable harmony emerges, inviting us to "believe that Jesus is the Christ, the Son of God; and that believing [we] might have life through his name" (John 20:31).

THE PSALM OF MARY, OR MARY'S MAGNIFICAT

WRITTEN BY TAYLOR HALVERSON, PhD,
AND LISA HALVERSON, PhD

"MY SOUL DOTH MAGNIFY THE LORD."

Thus spake the virgin Mary upon hearing of her grand calling to be the mother of the Savior of the world. Her willingness to submit to the will of the Father and to magnify Him is one that any one of us can hope to emulate in our own ways. And the song of praise that seems to burst forth from this young woman (see Luke 1:46–55) is one of the purest and humblest passages in all scripture.

The entire passage is referred to as the *Magnificat*, after the first word of the Latin canticle *Magnificat anima mea Dominum, et exultavit spiritus meus in Deo salutari meo*. In it, Mary speaks of the true nature of God and teaches us the correct way to respond to Him. When we look closely at the passage, each phrase is instructive. Moreover, each one is echoed in other scripture.

Let's journey through Mary's ten verses and several other scriptures of a similar nature. In doing so we can come closer to Mary's understanding of God the Father and thus, like her, more readily trust in His power.

46 And Mary said,
   My soul doth magnify the Lord
>   *My soul delighteth to prophesy concerning [the Savior], for I have seen his day, and my heart doth magnify his holy name.* (2 Nephi 25:13)
>   *Let your light so shine before this people, that they may see your good works, and glorify your Father who is in heaven.* (3 Nephi 12:16)

And whatsoever thing ye shall ask in my name, that will I do,
　　that the Father may be glorified in the Son. (John 14:13)

47　And my spirit hath rejoiced in the Lord my Savior.
And Hannah prayed, and said, My heart rejoiceth in the Lord,
　　mine horn is exalted in the Lord . . . ; I rejoice in thy salvation
　　There is none holy as the Lord. (1 Samuel 2:1–2)
And we talk of Christ, we rejoice in Christ, we preach of Christ,
　　we prophesy of Christ, and we write according to our prophesies,
　　that our children may know to what source they may look
　　for a remission of their sins. (2 Nephi 25:26)

48　For he hath regarded the low estate of his handmaiden:
And [Hannah] said, O Lord of hosts, if thou wilt indeed look on the
　　affliction of thine handmaiden, and remember me, and not forget
　　thine handmaid, but wilt give unto thine handmaid a man
　　child, then I will give him unto the Lord all the days of his life.
　　(1 Samuel 1:11)
The Lord . . . inviteth them all to come unto him and partake of his
　　goodness, and he denieth none that come unto him, black and
　　white, bond and free, male and female . . . ; and all are alike
　　unto God. . . . (2 Nephi 26:33)

Learn of me, for I am meek and lowly of heart. (Matthew 11:29)

for, behold, from henceforth all generations shall call me blessed.
Who can find a virtuous woman? For her price is far above rubies . . . .
　　Her children arise up, and call her blessed; her husband also. . . .
　　A woman that feareth the Lord, she shall be praised.
　　(Proverbs 31:10, 28, 30)
And the angel came in unto [Mary], and said, Hail, thou virgin, who art
　　highly favored of the Lord. The Lord is with thee, for thou art
　　chosen and blessed among women. (JST Luke 1:28)
Elizabeth was filled with the Holy Ghost; and she spake out with a loud
　　voice, and said, Blessed art thou among women, and blessed is
　　the fruit of thy womb. (Luke 1:42)

> *She [the woman who anointed Christ with oil] hath done what she*
> *could: and this which she has done unto me, shall be had in*
> *remembrance in generations to come, wheresoever my gospel shall*
> *be preached; for verily she has come beforehand to anoint my body to*
> *the burying.* (JST Mark 14:8)

49 For he that is mighty had done great things;

> *Then was our mouth filled with laughter, and our tongue with singing:*
> *then said they among the heathen, The Lord hath done great things*
> *for them.* (Psalms 126:2)
>
> *Yea, how is it that ye have forgotten what great things the Lord hath done*
> *for us . . . , and how it is that ye have forgotten that the Lord is able*
> *to do all things according to his will, for the children of men, if they*
> *exercise faith   in him? Wherefore, let us be faithful unto him.* (1
> Nephi 7:11–12)
>
> *By small and simple things are great things brought to pass; and small*
> *means in many instances doth confound the wise. And the Lord God*
> *doth work by means to bring about his great and eternal purposes.*
> (Alma 37:6–7)

and holy is his name.

> *Let them praise thy great and terrible name, for it is holy.* (Psalms
> 99:3)
>
> *Our Father which are in heaven, Hallowed be thy name.* (Matthew
> 6:9)
>
> *Who shall not fear thee, O Lord, and glorify thy name?*
> *For thou only art holy.* (Revelation 15:4)

50 And his mercy is on them that fear him from generation to generation.

> *Gather me the people together, and I will make them hear my words,*
> *that they may learn to fear me all the days that they shall live upon*
> *the earth, and that they may teach their children.* (Deuteronomy
> 4:10)
>
> *The Lord is merciful and gracious, slow to anger, and plenteous in mercy.*
> *. . . For as the heaven is high above the earth, so great is his mercy*
> *toward them that fear him. . . . The mercy of the Lord is from*
> *everlasting to everlasting upon*

them that fear him, and his righteousness unto children's children.
(Psalms 103:8-17)

51 He hath showed strength with his arm;

*Awake, awake, put on strength, O arm of the Lord. . . . The Lord hath
made bare his holy arm in the eyes of all the nations; and all the ends
of the earth shall see the salvation of our God.* (Isaiah 51:9; 52:10)

*And [Jesus] took [the little children] up in his arms, put his hands upon
them, and blessed them.* (Mark 10:16)

*The Lord hath redeemed my soul from hell; I have beheld his glory, and I
am encircled about eternally in the arms of his love.* (2 Nephi 1:15)

he hath scattered the proud in the imagination of their hearts.

*For, behold, the day cometh, that shall burn as an oven; and all the
proud, yea, and all that do wickedly, shall be stubble: and the day
that cometh shall burn them up, saith the Lord of hosts, that it shall
leave them neither root nor branch.* (Malachi 4:1)

52 He hath put down the mighty from their seats,

*But it must need be done in mine own way; and behold this is the way
that I, the Lord, have decreed to provide for my saints, that the poor
shall be exalted, in that the rich are made low.* (D&C 104:16)

and exalted them of low degree.

*And Jesus went into the temple of God, and cast out all them that
sold and bought in the temple, and overthrew the tables of the money-
changers, and the seats of them that sold doves, and said unto them,
It is written, My house shall be called the house of prayer; but ye have
made it a den of thieves. And the blind and the lame came to him in
the temple; and he healed them.* (Matthew 21:12–13)

*But he that is greatest among you shall be your servant. And whosoever
shall exalt himself shall be abased; and he that shall humble himself
shall be exalted.* (Matthew 23:11–12)

53 He hath filled the hungry with good things;

*And he took the seven loaves, and gave thanks, and brake, and gave
to his disciples to set before them; and they did set them before the*

*people. And   they had a few small fishes; and he blessed, and
commanded to set them also before them. So they did eat,
and were filled. . . .* (Mark 8:6–8)
*And blessed are they who do hunger and thirst after righteousness, for
they shall be filled with the Holy Ghost.* (3 Nephi 12:6)
*And he said unto them: He that eateth this bread eateth of my body
to his soul; and he that drinketh of this wine drinketh of my
blood to his soul; and his soul shall never thirst, but shall be filled.* (3
Nephi 20:8)

and the rich he hath sent empty away.
*And behold, one came and said unto him, Good Master, what good thing
shall I do, that I may have eternal life? . . . Jesus said unto him, If
thou wilt be perfect, go and sell that thou hast, and give to the poor,
and thou shalt have treasure in heaven: and come and follow me. But
when the young man heard that saying, he went away sorrowful: for
he had great possessions.* (Matthew 19:16, 21–22)

54 He hath helped his servant Israel, in remembrance of his mercy.
*Thou wilt perform the truth to Jacob, and the mercy to Abraham, which
thou has sworn unto our fathers from the days of old.* (Micah 7:20)

55 As he spake to our fathers, to Abraham, and to his seed for ever.
*Blessed be the Lord God of Israel; for he hath visited and redeemed
his people. . . . To perform the mercy promised to our fathers,
and to remember his holy covenant; The oath which he sware to
our father Abraham. . . .* (Luke 1:68, 72–73)

As did Mary, may we each seek to magnify the Lord and to rejoice
in our Savior. May we have faith in the Father's ability to do great and
blessed things in our own lives. May we trust in His word, His justice,
and His mercy. In doing so, we will find that we are filled with good
things and with a greater testimony of God our Eternal Father.

MATTHEW 11 AND LUKE 7, 11-13: COMING UNTO CHRIST AND LEARNING OF HIM

"He descended below all things, in that he comprehended all things, that he might be in all and through all things, the light of truth."
(D&C 88:6)

CHRIST CAME TO SAVE US from our sins. He came to show us by word and deed how we might live lives of joy and happiness, despite the afflictions we all experience, so that we might taste the bitter and know to prize the sweet. His invitation is simple yet profound: "Come unto me. . . . Take my yoke upon you, and learn of me. . . . For my yoke is easy, and my burden is light" (Matthew 11:28–30).

Let's learn from Christ how He has exemplified this invitation. First, let's seek to understand the meaning of the invitation, and second, let's review several New Testament stories that demonstrate the yoke of Christ.

COME UNTO ME

At the heart of Christ's saving work is His invitation to come to Him, to be embraced in His loving arms, and to be healed of all our sins. But notice that *we* are the ones who are to move; we are the ones who are to act. Christ cannot save us if we are not willing. Christ cannot save us if we do not come unto Him. To illustrate, let's look at this phrase from a different perspective (that of a different language).

On my mission, only after many mistakes and the kind help of others was I able to properly express myself in the Spanish language. For example, it was common for us as missionaries to invite people to church. In the English language we simply say, "Come to church." Making a straight translation into Spanish, I would say, *"Venga a la iglesia"* ("Come to the church"). Usually people gave me a funny look but kindly nodded, which I interpreted as indicating that they were agreeing to go to church. In reality they were probably thinking, *Ah, you are one of those silly gringos who doesn't know how to speak Spanish!* I soon discovered I had been making a grammatical error. In Spanish, you cannot invite someone to come to a certain location *unless you are already there.* For example, if I am at my friend's home I can tell my friend to "go to church," but I cannot say "come to church" because I am not *at* the church. However, if I was *at* the church and called my friend at his home I could rightly say, "Come to church," because I am already there.

How does this apply to Christ's invitation, "Come to me"? *Christ is already there!* He is where *we* want to be. He is already in the place *He* wants us to be. He is at the center. He is the focus, and He is the place. It is as though we are out in the dark and dreary wilderness, and He is in the celestial room of the temple calling us to come to Him. And if we are willing, we can turn our hearts, our minds, and our souls to Him. With His loving guidance and strength, we can move to where He is.

TAKE MY YOKE UPON YOU

To better understand this phrase, let's delve into the Greek of the New Testament and the ancient Mediterranean world. The word *yoke* comes from the Greek word *zugos,* and it is used in a variety of contexts. It can refer to balances or scales, such as those used by merchants or those that symbolize justice (a relevant reference is Revelation 6:5). In the context of Matthew 11:29, it can refer to a heavy crossbeam, which is a metaphor for being bound in slavery to a heavy load.

Zugos is also quite common throughout the Greek Old Testament. What do we mean by Greek Old Testament and where did it come from? Let's provide some context. Alexander the Great conquered the Middle East around 332 BC and brought an infusion of Greek culture and language to the Middle East. After a generation or two there were many Jews who spoke only Greek as their native tongue. Since they still wanted to be able to read their sacred scriptures, those works were translated from Hebrew to Greek. The situation of Greek-cultured Jews is comparable to that of most Bible readers today. Those of us who do not know the original languages of the Bible (such as Hebrew) rely gratefully on good translations into our native tongue, such as the King James Version for

English speakers. Around 275 BC, the resulting Greek translation of the Hebrew Old Testament was completed; it was called the Septuagint (The Greek Old Testament). The Septuagint is often referred to as LXX, the Roman numerals for 70, because tradition maintains that seventy Jewish elders translated the Hebrew Bible into Greek in just seventy days, a stunning miracle.

We find the word *zugos* in many passages of the Septuagint, which offers us interesting insights. For example, *zugos* is often used in the Septuagint to refer to the tyrannical and oppressive rule of foreign powers over Israel. Similarly, God speaks of breaking oppressive yokes and delivering His people (see Leviticus 26:13; Isaiah 9:3, 10:27, 11:13, 14:5, 25). Remember that these references are based on the Greek Old Testament (Septuagint) translation. The English translations, such as the King James Version, may not necessarily have the exact English word *yoke* but instead may have other related words.

On the other hand, *zugos* is also used in the Septuagint to refer to the "yoke of God"—or, in other words, to covenant fidelity to God's commandments and His everlasting grace. But as we have witnessed all too often, the natural man desires to be "free" of all constraints and all yokes. Thus even the yoke of God, which is to be easy and light, is rejected (see Jeremiah 2:20; 5:5).[7]

Christ's Yoke

During the life of Christ there were many different sects of Judaism, just as today there are many sects (or denominations) of Christianity. (Christianity in its original context was another sect of Judaism). One sect of Judaism during Christ's day was Pharisaic Judaism. The Pharisees were zealous for upholding both the written and oral law of Moses. We have today the written law of Moses recorded in the Bible's first five books of Moses le. The oral law was those practices, beliefs, and traditions attributed to Moses that some Jews handed down over many generations via word of mouth. In reality, most of these beliefs and observations were things preferred by certain practicing Jews, particularly those who adhered to Pharisaic Judaism. The Sadducees (another sect of Judaism)

---

[7] Gerhard Kittel, ed., *Theological Dictionary of the New Testament (TDNT)*, Geoffrey W. Bromiley, trans. and ed., Vol. 2 (Grand Rapids, MI: Wm. B. Eerdmans Publishing Company, 1999), 896–901.

had many warm disputes with the Pharisees over these oral-law traditions, as did Jesus. So it is clear from the New Testament record that not all Jews believed that the oral law was revealed by God.

Many of these oral-law traditions were unnecessary and burdensome. In some instances, such oral-law traditions precluded doing that which is good, which is ultimately the law of God. So in Christ's time, many of the Jewish people were burdened with an oppressive yoke of servitude to so-called laws and ordinances that did not come from God but were being taught as though they *did* come from God. In reality, the laws and covenants of God, though a type of yoke, will lighten us from servitude to the things of this world, to sin, and to the natural man. Thus, Christ invites all of us to drop the yoke of false traditions and beliefs and instead bind ourselves to Him in covenant and wear the yoke of His discipleship, which leads to life and salvation.

Nephi of old understood this mighty principle when he exclaimed, "And now, my beloved brethren, seeing that our merciful God has given us so great knowledge concerning these things, let us remember him, and lay aside our sins, and not hang down our heads, for we are not cast off" (2 Nephi 10:20).

LEARN OF ME

The underlying Greek word for *learn* is *manthano*, which can mean several things: (1) learning through instruction, (2) learning through inquiry, and (3) learning through practice.[8] Christ does indeed teach us through instruction, and if we are desirous, we can learn marvelous truths through inquiry:

> And if thou wilt inquire, thou shalt know mysteries which are great and marvelous; therefore thou shalt exercise thy gift, that thou mayest find out mysteries, that thou mayest bring many to the knowledge of the truth. (D&C 6:11)

One of the most important ways for us to learn is by practice. This life is the time for us to prepare to return to God's presence. Every day we have numerous opportunities to prepare by practicing gospel principles. If we err, the Atonement of Christ can save us, if we repent.

---

[8] Timothy and Barbara Friberg, *Friberg Analytical Lexicon to the Greek New Testament* (2000), *manthano*.

MY YOKE IS EASY AND MY BURDEN IS LIGHT

After studying the significance of the word *yoke*, let's explore these parallel statements:

My	yoke	is	easy
My	burden	is	light

Christ tells us that His yoke is *easy*. Great significance and meaning is packed into the Greek word for *easy*, which is *chrestos*. (Don't confuse this word with the similar-sounding Greek word *christos*, which means "anointed".) This word is used to refer to something that has a good or excellent purpose or pleasant requirements. It is also used comparatively for something that is better or superior to something else; it would be like saying the law of God (the yoke of Christ) is superior (more excellent and pleasant) than the law of Pharisaic Judaism (law of oral tradition).[9]

Greek *chrestos* can also refer to loving-kindness and mercy, comparable to the Hebrew word *hesed*. Thus when Christ says that His yoke is easy, He is telling us that it is suitable for excellent and virtuous purposes (such as salvation) and that the yoke will bind us to His everlasting kindness and mercy.

The word parallel to "easy" is *light*. That word further emphasizes that Christ's commandments and His way of living is easier—less of a burden—than false traditions and beliefs, and that it is also a much lighter burden than the oppressiveness of sin.

Let's discover in the scriptures how Christ taught in word and deed that His yoke is easy and His burden light.

DOING GOOD ON THE SABBATH DAY

Matthew 12:1–13 and Luke 13:10–17 comprise three stories that have one central purpose: to teach that the works of God (good deeds) are lawful on the Sabbath and that the oppressive yoke of false traditions can preclude us from doing righteousness. Thus if we follow the example of Christ and take His yoke upon us, we too will do that which is good, such as feeding the hungry, clothing the naked, relieving the sick and afflicted, comforting those who mourn, and visiting the lonely, even if those things defy social customs or traditions.

---

[9] Friberg, *chrestos*.

Harvesting on the Sabbath (Matthew 12:1–9)

In this first story, the Pharisees complained to the Savior that His disciples had profaned the Sabbath by plucking ears of corn, rubbing them in their hands, and eating. We read in the Old Testament that the law of Moses did make a statement about plucking ears of corn: "When thou comest into the standing corn of thy neighbor, then thou mayest pluck the ears with thine hand; but thou shalt not move a sickle unto thy neighbour's standing corn" (Deuteronomy 23:25).

The disciples, then, were not in violation of this particular law of Moses. However, according to Pharisaic *interpretation*—remember that the oral-law tradition was simply an interpretative tradition—they were in violation of another law of Moses: "Six days thou shalt work, but on the seventh day thou shalt rest: in earing time and in harvest thou shalt rest" (Exodus 34:21).

The Pharisees interpreted the act of plucking corn, rubbing it in your hands, and eating it as harvesting, and thus they accosted Jesus. Later Rabbinic tradition states that plucking is reaping (see *Mishnah Shabbat* 7:2). But in His masterfulness, Jesus taught them the oppressiveness of their unnecessary traditions and yokes. He reminded the Pharisees of the example of David, who ate the shewbread of the temple when he was hungry. The shewbread was sacred bread set upon a special table in the holy precincts of the temple and dedicated to God. Only consecrated priest were authorized to partake of this bread. But at one point David was extremely hungry, and all that was available was the temple showbread, so he ate it. This would be akin to an extremely hungry person asking for something to eat when all we had to offer them was the leftover sacrament bread. In this situation, feeding the hungry, even with the sacred bread of the sacrament, is the greater good.

As if this was not strong enough reasoning, Christ then used the example of the priests performing sacrifices at the temple on the Sabbath. Performing sacrifices was doing work, and someone could claim that they profaned the Sabbath—but theirs was a holy work.

Christ then went further in His reasoning. He testified that He is greater than the temple; He also testified that ultimately mercy is greater than sacrifice. Thus if the temple sacrifices are a greater good than Sabbath observance, and if mercy is greater than sacrifice, then it is a greater good to have mercy on hungry disciples who are with the One who Himself is greater than the temple. Ultimately, Christ is the Law, and he is the Lord of the Sabbath. No amount of peculiar observances or traditions will bring souls closer to Christ unless they come from the Lord Himself.

Healing on the Sabbath: Example 1 (Matthew 12:10–13)

In another brilliant episode that displays the blindness of refusing to do good works on the Sabbath, Christ entered a synagogue to teach how we might take His yoke upon us by doing that which is good. In the presence of all, Christ healed a man with a lame hand. Then to teach the lesson of the yoke of righteousness, he explained that if it is lawful on the Sabbath to deliver a domestic animal trapped in a pit, then indeed it is lawful to deliver a human soul. Because a human soul is more valuable than that of an animal, it is lawful to extract a person from the pit, whether that pit be physical challenges, sin, social oppression, or some other kind of tyranny.

Healing on the Sabbath: Example 2 (Luke 13:10–17)

In a similar story of healing, Christ entered a certain synagogue one Sabbath. Finding there a woman who had been physically suffering for more than eighteen years, He laid hands on her and commanded that the infirmity depart.

The laying on of hands is a representation of power and strength conveyed from one individual to another. Christ, the Author of all creation, has the power to heal all things. His are the hands of healing. Even the mere touch of the hem of His robe conveyed sufficient power to heal a woman who had been bleeding for many years.

In the example at the synagogue, Christ placed His hands of power on the woman, and she was made straight. What does *straight* mean? It comes from the Greek word *anortho'o*, which means "to restore," "to strengthen," "to rebuild," or simply "to make straight," as in this passage.[10] Christ is the great Restorer who has the power to make our weaknesses strengths and to rebuild that which we thought was lost.

THE HEALING BALM OF FORGIVENESS (Luke 7:31–50)

Lest we misunderstand, we should be careful not to paint Christ in an adversarial relationship with all of the Pharisees. For example, in

---

[10] Barclay M. Newman, Jr., *A Concise Greek-English Dictionary of the New Testament* (Deutsche Bibelgesellschaft [German Bible Society]: Stuttgart, 1993), *anortho'o*.

Luke 7:31–50, Christ dines with a certain Pharisee named Simon. In this context, Christ once again shows forth His merciful healing power and exemplifies what it means to carry His yoke.

During this time period, some of the Jewish dining practices were borrowed from the larger Greco-Roman cultural environment, just like many Mormons today tend to follow the dining practices of the nations and communities in which they reside. It that ancient time, it was common for individuals to gather reclining around a low-lying table; their feet would be extended out away from the table. At this particular meal, a penitent woman entered and washed Christ's feet and anointed them with ointment. In that day, ointments were used for various circumstances: (1) cosmetic for festive occasions, (2) funerary, (3) medicinal, or (4) ritual. Such a gift must have been costly, for alabaster (akin to marble) was a highly prized possession and was quite expensive.

Additionally, the act of washing a guest's feet was one of the greatest acts of hospitality. Christ rightly rebuked Simon, who had not offered such hospitality but who had rather silently condemned the "sinful" woman who did. Christ then delivered a memorable parable on the power of forgiveness, showing that those who have the greatest need of forgiveness will love the most. We also see in this story the truth that the Atonement is real only for those who are real. In other words, only those who recognize their sins, only those who acknowledge their weakness, only those who turn to the Lord can partake of the expiating power of the Atonement. Those who seek to hide their sins, those who deny their weaknesses and put forward a false appearance, or those who act as those they have no need for the Atonement in the end cannot partake of the Atonement. They have denied reality. They have denied the truth, and they have failed to be true and real. And thus the Atonement cannot be real for them because they have not been real.

CONCLUSION

Christ invites us to be equally yoked with Him. He knows all of our trials, sufferings, and difficulties. He has condescended below all things that He might be in all things and comprehend all things. Because He perfectly comprehends us, He can fully share our burdens. Yet Christ did not come to just share our burdens; He came to invite us to put aside our burdens and instead share *His* burden, *His* yoke.

When we heed His invitation to come unto Him, when we take His yoke upon us, the worldly, sinful burdens that we carry are purged and we are bound in everlasting covenants to our Creator. We then carry together with Him the "burden" of living the gospel principles, of spreading goodness and righteousness across the earth. We find the enlivening joy of purifying peace offered only through the Atonement.

The Atonement is a gracious gift to us when we are bound to God in covenant fidelity. Then the promises of Christ's everlasting kindness and mercy will be ours, and our burdens truly will be light.

LUKE 4–6 AND MATTHEW 10: FAITHFULLY RESPONDING TO GOD'S CALL

INTRODUCTION

EARLY CHAPTERS OF THE GOSPELS share various aspects of Jesus Christ's divine mission: Messianic prophecies, glorious birth, precocious youth, exemplary baptism, and the spread of gospel truths. Christ was not to be alone in His mission, however, except in His suffering. So we turn to the events surrounding Christ's public proclamation of His mission, the call of the Twelve Apostles, and the preparation they received to follow in His footsteps. In doing so, we'll see that Christ taught His Apostles by example how to be true disciples engaged in the work of righteousness.

CHRIST PUBLICLY PROCLAIMS HIS MESSIANIC MISSION

To begin, let's listen to Luke's testimony. As Luke 4 opens, we find Jesus in a mighty spiritual exercise of fasting for forty days and nights. After masterfully overcoming diverse forms of temptations, He was "endued" with spiritual power and returned to Galilee to proclaim His ministry. *Endued*, or endowed, comes from the Greek term ενδυω (*enduo*), which means "to clothe."

On one particular Sabbath, Christ gathered at the synagogue with other Jews in His boyhood town of Nazareth to read and expound on the scriptures as was the custom. The term *synagogue* derives from the Greek term συναγωγη (*sunagogay*), which means "assembly, congregation, gathering." The synagogue was

> the meeting place and prayer hall of the Jewish people since antiquity. During later Second Temple times [c. 580 BC–70 AD] the term "synagogue" referred both to a group of people

and/or a building or institution. Although these notions are not mutually exclusive, it is quite probable that at its inception the synagogue did not refer to an actual building but to a group or community of individuals who met together for worship and religious purposes. . . . By the 1st century [AD] the synagogue had become so important and central an institution to Jewish life in Palestine that the Talmud of Palestine refers to 480 of them existing in Jerusalem at the time of Vespasian [c. 70 AD]. . . . Josephus [the ancient Jewish author and historian who lived from 37 AD–105 AD] also emphasizes the centrality of the reading of Scripture and the importance of study found in the Second Temple synagogue. . . . The [New Testament] corroborates such a picture in reporting Jesus' and Paul's frequent visitations to synagogues. During those times they would invariable read or expound Scripture. . . . The origin of the synagogue is shrouded in mystery, though most scholars would place its beginning in exilic times. . . . It was the destruction of the Jerusalem temple in 587/6 [BC] and the forced eviction of Judeans to Babylonia that created the conditions which brought about a complete reappraisal of life. . . . Another aspect of the life crisis facing the Judeans in exile was the question of how to worship without a sanctuary located on a holy place. . . . Whatever the reality of the situation in exile, the fact of the matter is that the response to Cyrus' edict in 538 [BC] permitting the Judeans to return to Palestine was underwhelming. Many chose to stay in the Persian diaspora and such a decision clearly indicates that their religious needs were being met. . . . Whatever the case may be for an exilic date for the idea or actual establishment of the synagogue as a place where individuals gathered to worship, read, or recite the scriptures, and to venerate [God], the experience and trauma of the destruction and exile of God's people enabled the Judeans to develop a means of approaching God that transcended the confines of sacred space.[11]

---

[11] David Noel Freedman, ed., *Anchor Bible Dictionary* (New York: Doubleday, 1992), 6:251–252.

When the scrolls came to where Jesus was seated, He stood, opened to a passage in Isaiah, and in great solemnity read a Messianic prophecy. Luke identifies Isaiah 61:1–2 as the passage that Jesus read. In the Gospel of Luke, the name of Isaiah is written as "Esaias." Why? We remember that Luke was likely a Gentile, since he was educated in the Greek educational system, and he was probably writing to a Greek-speaking audience. More than likely the version of the Old Testament that Luke referred to was the Greek Septuagint (and as mentioned earlier, often symbolized with the Latin numbers for seventy as LXX). Hence, Isaiah's name was written in Greek as "Esaias." We shouldn't be surprised, however, for even Isaiah today would not recognize his own name pronounced in English, since "Isaiah" is simply the English version of the Hebrew name *Yeshayahu*. According to tradition, the Septuagint (LXX) was translated by Jews from Hebrew into Greek around 275 BC in the city of Alexandria, Egypt. For Greek-speaking Jews (and later for Greek-speaking Christians), the Septuagint (LXX) became the standard Old Testament version, much like the King James Version is the standard Old Testament version for English-speaking Mormons.

Let's compare Luke's version of the Messianic prophecy Jesus read with that of Isaiah. A careful examination of these two passages will reveal powerful insights to Christ's purpose and ministry. Isaiah's version is on the left (with differences highlighted in *italics*), and Luke's version is on the right (with differences highlighted in **bold**).

Isaiah 61:1-3	Luke 4:18-19
1 The Spirit of the Lord *GOD* is upon me; because *the LORD* hath anointed me to preach *good tidings unto* the *meek*; he hath sent me to *bind up* the brokenhearted, to *proclaim liberty* to the captives, and *the opening of* the *prison* to them that are *bound;*	18 The Spirit of the Lord is upon me, because **he** hath anointed me to preach the **gospel to** the **poor**; he hath sent me to **heal** the brokenhearted, to **preach deliverance** to the captives, and **recovering of sight to** the **blind,** to **set at liberty** them that are **bruised,**
2 To *proclaim* the acceptable year of the LORD, and the day of vengeance of our God; to comfort all that mourn;	19 To **preach** the acceptable year of the Lord.
3 To appoint unto them that mourn in Zion, to give unto them beauty for ashes, the oil of joy for mourning, the garment of praise for the spirit of heaviness; that they might be called trees of righteousness, the planting of the LORD, that he might be glorified.	

In Isaiah 61:1, the reference to Deity is "Lord God," whereas in Luke's version it is simply "Lord." In the Old Testament, any reference to "Lord God" is written in the Hebrew as *Adonai Jehovah. Jehovah*, or more precisely, *Yahweh*, was the divine name not to be uttered. At first take, we may think that such a small change is of no importance, but this one is.

Consider the Jewish prohibition against uttering the divine name of God. According to the New Testament, Jews during the time of Jesus were quite particular about blasphemy, a sin they considered punishable by death. Even the mere mention of God's name could be grounds for blasphemy. Then how did one avoid getting himself killed while reading the scriptures in the synagogue, particularly when the great prophet Isaiah regularly wrote out in entirety the name "Lord God"? One simply said, as Jesus appropriately did in the synagogue, "Lord" (*Adonai*) instead of "Lord God" (*Adonai Jehovah*).

The other changes in the accounts are also quite significant and mutually support each other in a rich expression of gospel truths. Look how the changes are different yet parallel and complimentary. Again, the Isaiah version is on the left while Luke's parallel statements are on the right:

Isaiah 61:1	Luke 4:18
Good tidings	Gospel
Meek	Poor
Bind up	Heal
Proclaim liberty	Preach deliverance
	Recovering of sight to the blind
The opening of the prison	Set at liberty
Bound	Bruised
Proclaim	Preach

What we notice here is that Jesus is keeping with the spirit of Isaiah's message yet slightly altering the words to give additional depth and richness, which helps Him express His merciful mission of loving kindness. One aspect Jesus did add that is not found in the Isaiah passage is mention of giving sight to the blind. This Christ did, and not just in physical terms, though He did that as well (see, for example, Matthew 9:27–31 and Mark 8:22–26). Christ also came to heal spiritual blindness. He came to open our eyes to our own weaknesses that by seeing them we might be free through repentance and the purging fire of forgiveness (see Ether 12:27).

Let's now return to the account of Christ publicly announcing Himself in the synagogue. After He finished reading the Isaiah passage, what happened next is riveting:

And he closed the book, and he gave *it* again to the minister, and sat down. And the eyes of all them that were in the synagogue were fastened on him. And he began to say unto them, This day is this scripture fulfilled in your ears. And all bare him witness, and wondered at the gracious words which proceeded out of his mouth. And they said, Is not this Joseph's son? (Luke 4:20–22)

The immensity of what was announced that day was beyond the comprehension or acceptance of those in that Nazareth synagogue. Jesus was but a carpenter's son in an obscure Galilean village on the fringes of the enormous Roman Empire. How could the long anticipation of mighty prophetic fulfillment come to one who was so . . . so meek?

Perceiving their unbelief, Jesus continued to speak, but in parables. He also reminded them that "no prophet is accepted in his own country" (Luke 4:24), and He likened Himself to the great healing, preaching, and miracle performing prophets of Old Testament times, namely Elijah and Elisha. *Elias* is the Greek form of the name "Elijah." This is again evidence that Luke writes in Greek and/or his audience reads Greek and that they use as their standard Old Testament, the Greek Septuagint (LXX). *Eliseus* was the Greek form of the name "Elisha." As with the Savior, these two prophets also were persecuted and not well accepted even among their own people. In fact, some of their greatest works had been done among the "Gentiles." For example, Elijah ensured that a Sidonian widow would have enough to eat during a famine; Elisha healed the leprosy of Syrian Naaman. Despite opposition and rejection from their own people to whom they were to minister, these two Israelite prophets were true to their commission from God and were rewarded with the blessings of heaven.

Not one word of truth penetrated the hearts of Jesus's listeners that day in Nazareth. In wrath they rose up against Jesus to destroy Him. But like Nephi, son of Helaman, in the Book of Mormon (Helaman 10:16), He was conveyed out of their midst. And taking His journey He went "to Capernaum, a city of Galilee, and taught [the willing] on the sabbath days" (Luke 4:31).

CHRIST'S MINISTRY IN THE GALILEE

With great haste and excitement the message went abroad, "We have found him, of whom Moses in the law, and the prophets, did write, Jesus of Nazareth, the son of Joseph" (John 1:45). Though some doubted, like the Jews of Nazareth, with such words as, "Can there any good thing come out of Nazareth?" (John 1:46), the enthusiasm for the promised Messiah could not be abated. He was proclaimed with joyful shouts of "come and see!" (John 1:46).

The crowds pressed upon Him, both to hear His precious words and to be close to this source of healing. At one point Jesus had to use Peter Simon's fishing boat to launch Himself off the shore of the Sea of Galilee in order to teach the thronging multitudes (see Luke 5:1-3). This set the context for the formal calling of some of His Apostles, disciples who had been with Him in His early ministry and had beheld His marvelous works of everlasting kindness and mercy.

CALLING HIS APOSTLES

Ever the Master Teacher, Christ employed the seemingly mundane tasks of life as symbols of powerful principles and ideas. For example, He urged weary fisherman to cast forth their nets even though they had toiled throughout the night without success. To the amazement of all, their nets gathered in schools of fish to the point of breaking.

Some see this story as a symbol that Peter and the other future Apostles were not yet capable of spreading the gospel message entirely on their own. Then later, after several years of divine training with Christ, they could cast out their nets and bring in until overflowing without the nets breaking (see John 21). They were then ready to successfully take the message to the world.

When the fishermen-disciples saw the bounteous miracle of the fishes, they were filled with amazement. In simple, yet profoundly symbolic words, Christ said to them, "Fear not; from henceforth thou shalt catch men" (Luke 5:10). It required nothing more than to return to land for these devout men to forsake all and follow the Master (see Luke 5:11). What a marvelous example these simple men set. No sooner had they experienced one of the greatest success stories of their lives than they were asked in plain humility to forsake it *all*, and they did so *willingly*.

THE TUTORING BEGINS

Christ taught by example. His Apostles had been called to serve and live as He did, so Christ tutored them through His daily acts of loving kindness and spiritual self-mastery. For example, soon after Peter, Andrew, James, and John received their call to the Apostleship, Christ displayed His loving power to heal a man beset with the socially and physically debilitating disease of leprosy (see Luke 5:12–15). Then Christ retired to a secluded spot to pass the night in prayer (Luke 5:16). Through this simple act of worship, Christ taught His disciples that even the mighty Lord had need for communion with the Father. Indeed, prayer may have been a source for Christ's healing power.

As Christ's ministry progressed, opportunities to physically and spiritually heal those who came to Him were inextricably interwoven with the great work of teaching the people. All of this served as the tutoring context for His chosen Apostles as they accompanied him. With masterful grace, Christ answered the doubting and probing questioning from scribes and Pharisees who ever sought to find fault with the one who could save them from their faults, if they were only willing. For example, after telling a man with palsy that his sins were forgiven, Christ posed a question to the scribes and Pharisees: "Does it require more power to forgive sins than to make the sick rise up and walk?" (JST Luke 5:23). Christ answered His own question for these doubters by showing that He had power to do both. Under the command of God on earth and in the sight of all present, the man with palsy lept from his bed. Christ does have all power both in heaven and on earth to heal.

In this manner did Christ tutor His Apostles. By example He taught them that they were to show mercy, to heal, to teach, to liberate, and to protect.

PHYSICIAN FOR THE SICK

Levi, also known as Matthew, was a publican—a tax collector. Perhaps Matthew was collecting customs duties or taxes as a customs agent at the nearby provincial border. If Christ was attempting to win popular Pharisaic and scribal opinion, He certainly chose poorly with Matthew as an Apostle—and the opportunity soon arose for the self-righteous to make their opinions known. "Why do ye eat and drink with publicans and sinners?" they complained to Christ (Luke 5:30). In a rebuke that was gentle yet stinging, He replied, "They that are whole need not a physician; but they that are sick. I came not to call the righteous, but sinners to repentance" (Luke 5:31–31). In many of these interactions, Christ's Apostles were silent yet careful observers of the Lord's ministering work. Their time was not yet, but soon would be when they would have to answer similar inquiries from those who believed they had nothing to learn from the meek and chosen servants of God. But for the time being, they were under the tutelage of the Master of heaven and earth.

THE ANCIENT APOSTLES

Now who were these men that Christ especially chose? The names of those called to be special ministers for Christ in the dispensation of the Meridian of Times, according to the Gospel of Matthew, included these twelve:

Simon (also called Peter)
Andrew (brother to Peter)
James (son of Zebedee)
John (brother to James and son of Zebedee)
Philip
Bartholomew
Thomas
Matthew (the publican)
James (son of Alphaeus)
Lebaeus (also called Thaddaeus and also called Judas)
Simon (the Canaanite, also known as Simon the Zealot)
Judas (Iscariot)

THE MINISTRY OF APOSTLESHIP

Christ set forth the apostolic commission to the Twelve in Matthew chapter 10. The work that Christ ordained these men to undertake was by no means an easy task and was certainly not bedazzled with the glory of this world.

Provide neither gold, nor silver, nor brass in your purses, Nor scrip for your journey, neither two coats, neither shoes, nor yet staves: for the workman is worthy of his meat. . . . Behold, I send you forth as sheep in the midst of wolves: be ye therefore wise as serpents, and harmless as doves. But beware of men: for they will deliver you up to the councils, and they will scourge you in their synagogues; And ye shall be brought before governors and kings for my sake, for a testimony against them and the Gentiles. . . . And ye shall be hated of all men for my name's sake: but he that endureth to the end shall be saved. . . . And fear not them which kill the body, but are not able to kill the soul: but rather fear him which is able to destroy both soul and body in hell. (Matthew 10:9–10, 16–18, 22, 28)

However, the peace of Christ's Spirit was to ever accompany them, and the blessings of joy in this life and eternal joy in the life to come was the sure promise that Christ bestowed upon His Apostles as they set forth to accomplish their mighty tasks. They would not be left alone.

But when they deliver you up, take no thought how or what ye shall speak: for it shall be given you in that same hour what ye shall speak. For it is not ye that speak, but the Spirit of your Father which speaketh in you. . . . And fear not. . . . Are not two sparrows sold for a farthing? and one of them shall not fall on the ground without your Father. But the very hairs of your head are all numbered. Fear ye not therefore, ye are of more value than many sparrows. . . . And he that taketh not his cross, and followeth after me, is not worthy of me. He that findeth his life shall lose it: and he that loseth his life for my sake shall find it. (Matthew 10:19–20, 28–31, 38–39)

The Apostles received a specific commission to follow in the footsteps of the Savior's ministry. In so doing they would be blessed with the same power He had.

Go . . . to the lost sheep of the house of Israel. And as ye go, preach, saying, The kingdom of heaven is at hand. Heal the sick, cleanse the lepers, raise the dead, cast out devils: freely ye have received, freely give....And into whatsoever city or town ye shall enter, enquire who in it is worthy; and there abide till ye go thence. And when ye come into an house, salute it. And if the house be worthy, let your peace come upon it: but if it be not worthy, let your peace return to you. (Matthew 10:6–13)

CONCLUSION

The Apostles were then and are today special ministers of Christ's name unto all the world. Their commission has ever been the same throughout the ages of the world. Those who take upon themselves the name of Christ are invited to participate in sustaining that marvelous apostolic commission:

Go ye therefore, and teach all nations, baptizing them in the name of the Father, and of the Son, and of the Holy Ghost: Teaching them to observe all things whatsoever I have commanded you: and, lo, I am with you alway, *even* unto the end of the world. Amen. (Matthew 28:19–20)

WHO WERE THE SAMARITANS?

THERE WAS ONCE AN ANCIENT temple society led by hereditary high priests from the lineage of Levi who taught and transmitted the sacred words of God as preserved in the Torah (the five books of Moses). Each year at Passover, the community gathered in a solemn assembly to perform the rituals on the paschal lamb in remembrance that God had saved them from bondage. Through the years, this community worshiped God as Creator and Sustainer of all life. Yet this group was vilified and marginalized over the centuries—their beliefs mocked, their people scapegoated, and eventually their holy temple destroyed by outside forces. Their numbers have now dwindled to some four thousand active adherents.

But wait—are there not more than four thousand faithful Jews today? Absolutely! But we are not talking about the Jews; we are talking about the Samaritans! It can be easy to be confused: If we look closely, we discover that the Samaritans carry all of the important identifying features that would lead us to believe that they are faithful Israelites. Yet our scriptures tell us otherwise, and our popular lessons generalize them as mongrels, impure, and religiously vacuous.

Our view of the Samaritans is entirely shaped by the perspective that is offered to us—a perspective that is prevalent throughout both the Old and New Testament scriptures. How would our perspective and understanding of the Samaritans be enhanced if we heard their story through their own voices? How would this inform our understanding of the cultural and religious tensions that played an ongoing role in Palestinian society between the years of the Jewish return from exile to New Testament times (539 BC to 70 AD)?

Our present-day scriptures have preserved only the Jewish perspective of the origin and beliefs of the Samaritans. Thankfully, the Samaritans preserved their own version of their origin and beliefs. By reading the Jewish and Samaritan version side by side, we gain a fuller picture of the cultural and religious tensions active in Palestinian society over many centuries, enhancing our understanding of New Testament characters' interaction with Samaritans.

OUR PERSPECTIVE; THE JEWISH PERSPECTIVE

Before we listen to the authentic Samaritan voices, let's examine our own perspectives of the Samaritans and explore where these perspectives originated. Undoubtedly, we gain our understanding of the Samaritans from passages in the Old and New Testaments. What do they tell us?

We can begin by stepping back to 721 BC, when the Israelites were fractured into two kingdoms, the Northern Kingdom of ten tribes (also known as Israel, with its capital at Samaria) and the Southern Kingdom (also known as Judah, with its capital at Jerusalem). We remember at that time that the Israelites started a rebellion against the mighty Assyrian empire. Israel even tried to force Judah to join the revolt (see Isaiah 9). But Assyria conquered the Northern Kingdom's capital city of Samaria and deported nearly thirty thousand inhabitants to Mesopotamia. No one knows what happened to these people, but expectations have abounded over the centuries that the ten lost tribes would one day return.

However, not all of the Israelites of the Northern Kingdom were deported; many of the true Israelites remained. Yet the Jewish perspective on this matter urges us to see it differently. The Jewish account in 2 Kings 17:24–41 makes a strong claim that those "Israelites" left in Israel after the Assyrian conquest did not worship the Lord God, but instead perverted righteousness, practiced wickedness, and taught these things to their children.

Thus far, the story sounds familiar to us.

THE POWER OF THE JEWISH PERSPECTIVE ON THE SAMARITANS

The claims outlined in 2 Kings 17 were passed down so convincingly over the years that Jesus was able to use this Jewish perspective of the Samaritans as a powerful teaching tool when He delivered the simple but profound parable known as "The Good Samaritan" (see Luke 10).

How could Jesus teach the principle of being neighborly to even the most despicable people if His listeners didn't regard the people as despicable?

In contrast, Jesus, the Perfect Exemplar, showed utmost neighborliness to this downtrodden group by visiting them at the sacred well of Jacob (see John 4:5–26). Despite being caricatured as refuse and thus not even worth the effort of proselytizing, the Samaritans proved to be some of the most anxious to receive the "good news" that God's anointed Messiah had come (see John 4:39–42).

SAMARITAN VOICES SPEAK FROM THE DUST

Now that we've been reminded of where our perspective comes from, let's practice neighborliness by listening to the Samaritan side of the story.

Our best resources for understanding the Samaritans' own view of themselves derives from key records that they kept and transmitted. One of those is the Samaritan Pentateuch. They, like their Jewish relatives, highly regarded the words of God preserved in the first five books of the Bible or the Torah—so much so that the only work they accepted as scriptures were the five books of Moses. Today, by comparing the Hebrew Bible against the Samaritan Pentateuch, biblical scholars can detect word and grammar changes that suggest how the Samaritans understood and interpreted the scriptures.

The most important record for understanding the Samaritans from their perspective, however, is a document called *The Samaritan Chronicle*. This document claims that the Samaritans are true Israelites, descended from the tribes of Joseph (through Ephraim and Manasseh). In this document, the Samaritans also claim to have preserved the Holy Levitical Priesthood, preserved the correct forms of temple worship and sacrifice, guarded the purity of Israelite seed, and maintained true doctrines and beliefs, while Judah languished in sin and was corrupted by Babylonian exile. The Samaritans saw themselves as the true preservers of Israelite religion while the Jews lived according to an apostate and corrupted imitation of Mosaic practices.

Now that you have a general summary of the Samaritan documents, let's examine the primary documents from the Samaritan perspective. As you read, notice the way the Samaritans make use of familiar biblical characters (such as Eli, priest of the tabernacle and mentor to future prophet Samuel), ideas (such as the sacredness of the scriptures), and

institutions (such as temple worship and priesthood) in a narrative that is
not entirely familiar to us. Remember that their views are unfamiliar to us
because the Jewish perspective is the only one we have ever heard.

THE SAMARITAN CHRONICLE[12]

Explanatory and contextual information for the following is found in
the footnotes.

When the high priest Uzzi[13] took up the high priesthood in
succession to his fathers, there was a man named Eli[14] the son
of Jephunneh, of the descendants of Ithamar son of Aaron the
priest, as overseer of the House of Ithamar. This Eli sacrificed on
the altar of stones, and under his control was the entire revenue
of the Israelites' tithe which they offered to the Lord. He was a
prince over the whole tribe of Levi, under the command of the
high priest Uzzi. Now this Uzzi was but a youth, and Eli the son
of Jephunneh was well advanced in age. Eli yearned to take over
the position of the high priest Uzzi. . . . And the people of Israel
again did, at that time, what was evil in the sight of the Lord;
and furthermore Eli the son of Jephunneh was possessed of evil
designs, with the result that many of the Israelites turned from
the way of truth. He seduced them, and they took after idols,
formed marriage alliances with Gentiles,[15] and even gave their

[12] This translation is based on George W. E. Nickelsburg and Michael E. Stone, *Faith and Piety in Early Judaism: Texts and Documents* (Philadelphia: Fortress Press, 1983), 14–16.

[13] "According to Samaritan views, Uzzi was high priest in the true line of descent from Phineas, son of Eleazar, son of Aaron." *Faith and Piety in Early Judaism: Texts and Documents*, 15, f.n. a.

[14] This is the same Eli who took the young Samuel to the temple and helped him recognize the voice of the Lord. (See 1 Samuel 3.) What is significant about this entire Samaritan passage, which paints Eli in a bad light, is that the Samaritan perspective is entirely plausible given the evidence of Eli's fall from grace offered in 1 Samuel. See especially the Old Testament story of God rejecting Eli as high priest (see 1 Samuel 2: 35–36); Eli's sons (and heirs to the high priesthood) both die (see 1 Samuel 4:17). See also the story of Eli dying (see 1 Samuel 4:18).

[15] Notice how the Samaritans argue that the Jews were half-breeds. This is the same argument used by the Jews against the Samaritans. Some things just never change in religious and cultural wars (both sides use the same arguments against each other).

daughters to them; and they took the daughters of Gentiles as wives for themselves. . . .

Now Eli was ambitious, and he let it be known that he wanted to take over the position of high priest. . . . Eli won over to himself many of the Israelites by saying to them, "It is right that I should minister to a youth? I do not want such a status for myself, and I expect you to share my opinion and follow me." Eli went on to write to all the cities in the neighborhood of Mount Gerizim[16] Bethel, and he addressed the above words to them. These all gathered to his side and they addressed him as follows: "We accept what you have said; we will not disobey your orders. Everything you command us we will do." They made a covenant with him accordingly. . . .

At that particular time the Israelites who dwelt in the cities of Shechem, the cities of Philistia, and the cities of Jebus were divided in two. One side followed the high priest Uzzi the son of Bahqi, and the other followed Eli the son of Jephunneh. The latter became evil-minded, and they all followed their own inclinations. . . . The Josephites followed the high priest Uzzi the son of Bahqi, and the Judahites followed Eli the son of Jephunneh. The Ephraimites and Manassites drove out Eli and his community from the chosen place Mount Gerizim Bethel.[17]

Eli and his community, with their families and cattle, departed to sojourn in the territory of the tribe of Judah at Shiloh. Eli dwelt there in that place, and he made himself an ark of gold based on the structure of the ark of the testimony. He made himself also a mercy seat, cherubs, a table, a lampstand, and altars just like those of the sanctuary of Moses, which is to be found in the chosen place Mount Gerizim Bethel.

Eli wrote letters, sending them to the chief of the Israelites addressing them as follow: "Let whoever desires to see signs and wonders come to me at Shiloh, for the ark of the testimony containing the tablets is in my hands." He put into the ark the books of the law which were the version of Ithamar the son of

---

[16] Mount Gerizim, the holy mount where the Samaritans built their temple, is located about thirty miles to the North of Jerusalem.

[17] This is the location where the Samaritan temple stood for many years, and it is still the location where they gather on an annual basis to slaughter a paschal lamb for the Passover ritual. This is not far from the present-day Palestinian city of Nablus in the West Bank.

Eleazar son of Aaron the priest, peace be upon him. A good many Israelites gathered to him, and he built at Shiloh a tent based on the design of the tent of meeting.[18] This Eli did not change a single word of the holy law, but he revised the order of words.[19] Eli went on sacrificing the offerings on the altars which he had made. Everyone of his festivals was in accordance with the commandments of the holy law.[20]

CONTEXT OF RELIGIOUS AND CULTURAL WARS BETWEEN JEWS AND SAMARITANS (500 BC)

What is the context of such disputes? Some scholars have suggested that the key ingredients for these cultural and religious battles were the social conditions of the Jewish population returning from Babylonian exile as they came into contact with native inhabitants of Palestine.

In 539 BC, the Persian Empire, under command of Cyrus, conquered the Babylonians and liberated the many peoples—not just Jews—who had been living in exile. A true politician, Cyrus became the patron of each ethnic and religious group; just as the Jews were allowed to return to build their temple, so too were the Babylonians allowed to freely pursue their religious institutions, even though Cyrus adhered to neither of those religious systems. Cyrus was most likely part of the religious movement called Zoroastrianism. We know the story in part from the Bible as well as from the ancient "Cyrus Cylinder," which documents, from a Babylonian perspective, how Cyrus liberated the Babylonians from their own irreligious leader, thus allowing them to once again freely pursue their religious beliefs and practices.[21]

---

[18] The Samaritans are claiming that the Jewish temple and temple practices were apostate imitations.

[19] The Samaritans, who highly revere the scriptures, charge the Jews with textual tampering, thus destroying the credibility and power of the scriptures.

[20] For further reading on the Samaritans, see the following secondary sources: Alan D. Crown, ed., *The Samaritans* (Tubingen: J. C. B. Mohr, 1989); John Bowman, *The Samaritan Problem: Studies in the Relationships of Samaritanism, Judaism, and Early Christianity*, Alfred M. Johnson, Jr., trans. (Pittsburg: The Pickwich Press, 1975); R. J. Coggins, *Samaritans and Jews: The Origins of Samaritanism Reconsidered* (Oxford: Basil Blackwell, 1975); Ingrid Hjelm, *The Samaritans and Early Judaism: A Literary Analysis* (Sheffield: Sheffield Academic Press, 2000).

[21] See James B. Pritchard, ed., *The Ancient Near East: Volume 1—An Anthology of Texts and Pictures* (Princeton: Princeton University Press, 1958), 206–208.

The returning Jewish exiles saw themselves as the true Israelites, marching on their exodus out of Babylonian captivity much like their forebears had marched out of Egyptian captivity. Once back in the land of Palestine, the Jews tried to reestablish their customs, beliefs, and most importantly their temple practices with their attendant priesthood hierarchy, but other groups who claimed to be true Israelites (such as the Samaritans) wanted to participate. How were the returning exiles to determine who was truly Israel and who was not?

At first, amicable relations existed between the two groups (Jews and Samaritans) who both claimed to be the true Israel. In fact, one example of how amicable the relationship initially had been between the two groups is that a Jewish high priest, whose name was Manasses, had married the daughter of Sanballat, the Samaritan governor. It is interesting to note that Sanballat's name means "Sin gives life," *Sin* being the name of an Assyrian moon god. This name leads some to believe that the Samaritan Sanballat was truly an Assyrian emigrant. However, Sanballat certainly regarded himself as a true Israelite, even if his parents gave him an Assyrian name. He gave two of his own children Israelite names with the theophoric element of God's name (Jehovah/Yahweh = **iah**) in their name; Dela**iah** and Shelem**iah**. Even some prominent Jews had Babylonian/Mesopotamian names, such as Zerubbabel (which means "born in Babylon"). So the mere fact of having a foreign name does not mean that an individual is not truly of the house of Israel.[22]

But the peace did not last long.

This deterioration is outlined by Josephus, a Jewish historian living six hundred years after the initial controversy between the Jews and the Samaritans, which was sparked during the Persian period around 500 BC. Josephus, who lived from 37 AD to about 105 AD, wrote *The Antiquities of the Jews* around the year 95 AD. In it, Josephus relates the following story about the deteriorating relationship between the Samaritans and the Jews soon after the Babylonian exile:

> Now the elders of Jerusalem, resenting the fact that the brother [Manasses] of high priest Jaddus was sharing the high priesthood while married to a foreigner [Manasses was married

---

22 See *Anchor Bible Dictionary*, edited by David Noel Freedman (New York: Doubleday, 1992), 5:973-975.

to Nikaso, daughter of Samaritan governor Sanballat], rose up
against him, for they considered this marriage to be a stepping-
stone for those who might wish to transgress the laws about
taking wives and that this would be the beginning of intercourse
with foreigners. They believed, moreover, that their former
captivity and misfortunes had been caused by some who had
erred in marrying and taking wives who were not of their own
country. They therefore told Manasses either to divorce his
wife or not to approach the altar. And, as the high priest shared
the indignation of the people and kept his brother from the
altar, Manasses went to his father-in-law Sanaballetes [a variant
form of the name Sanballat] and said that while he loved his
daughter Nikaso, nevertheless the priestly office was the highest
in the nation and had always belonged to his family, and that
therefore he did not wish to be deprived of it on her account.
But Sanaballetes promised not only to preserve the priesthood
for him but also to procure for him the power and office of high
priest and to appoint him governor of all the places over which
he ruled, if he were willing to live with his daughter; and he said
that he would build a temple similar to that in Jerusalem on
Mount Garizein [This is a variant form of the name *Gerazim*,
sometimes also written *Gerizim*. This is the mountain upon which
the Samaritans built their temple and conducted sacrifices. This
is still the case today.]—this is the highest of the mountains near
Samaria—and undertook to do these things with the consent of
[Persian] King Darius. Elated by these promises, Manasses stayed
with Sanaballetes, believing he would obtain the high priesthood
as the gift of Darius, for Sanaballetes, as it happened, was now
an old man. But, as many priests and Israelites were involved
in such marriages [see Ezra 9], great was the confusion which
seized the people of Jerusalem. For all these deserted to Manasses,
and Sanaballetes supplied them with money and with land for
cultivation and assigned them places wherein to dwell, in every
way seeking to win favor for his son-in-law.[23]

---

[23] This translation comes from *Faith and Piety in Early Judaism: Texts and Documents*, 18–19.

The Samaritan and Jewish versions over who was true Israel is beginning to sound like two young siblings blaming the other for raiding the cookie jar (when all along both know that they each took a cookie).

What we see, then, is that both groups were attempting to show why they should be the legitimate Israel and thus heirs to the legitimate priesthood, to the legitimate scriptures, and to the legitimate temple. Interestingly, they shared similar yet competing stories. We must remember that in religious and cultural wars, some things never change (again, both sides use the same arguments against each other).

Who is right and who is wrong? That's not for us to decide. What we may discover in the end is that both the Jewish *and* the Samaritan stories have merit and truth to them. We can be assured that the Lord will work it all out in the end.

AFTERMATH OF THE JEWISH-SAMARITAN CONTROVERSY OF 500 BC

According to some leading Jews (such as Ezra and Nehemiah), the way to verify the true Israelites was through blood lineage, hence the focus on genealogies. Thus only those who could prove that they were of the literal house of Israel (of the pure blood) were allowed to participate in the religious and social customs that defined the Jewish community. Additionally, as Josephus reported above, some of the Jewish leaders feared that Jews mixing with the native inhabitants would lead to idolatry and wickedness, which they believed had been the reasons for the exile in the first place. Fearing a repeated disaster, leaders such as Ezra and Nehemiah created firm community boundaries and invoked the Mosaic law in Deuteronomy 23 against foreign marriages (see Nehemiah 13). The wall that Nehemiah had constructed around Jerusalem at this time may be a physical representation of this (see Nehemiah 2). Even then, Ezra still mourned over heedless Jews who did not follow the laws of God (see Ezra 9).

JEWS DESTROY THE SAMARITAN TEMPLE (128 BC)

About four hundred years after the initial controversy between Jews and Samaritans, the Maccabean Jews were the political and religious rulers over Palestine (about 167 BC). Working from a position of the old animosity as well as new controversies, the Jewish leader of that day, John

Hyrcanus, forcibly converted the Samaritans to Judaism and destroyed their temple, burning it to the ground in around 128 BC, much like the Romans burned the Jewish temple to the ground two hundred years later in 70 AD.

SAMARITANS IN THE NEW TESTAMENT

With this background context, we now have a richer perspective of the Jewish *and* Samaritan experience that informed their attitudes and world views during the New Testament times. Let's look at a few of the first instances of Jewish-Samaritan interactions/references in the New Testament and see if our new understanding sheds additional light on these passages.

Matthew 10:1–16

These verses focus on Jesus calling His Apostles and delivering to them their unique commission to preach the gospel. It is interesting to note that Jesus requests that the Apostles go *first* to the lost sheep of Israel and *later* to the Gentiles and Samaritans (see especially verse 5).

Luke 10:25–37

This chapter contains the famous parable known as "The Good Samaritan." We mentioned earlier that by leveraging the negative Jewish stereotypes of the Samaritans, Jesus was able to teach a powerful principle of brotherhood and neighborliness.

John 4:4–42

Even though Jesus explains that His main mission was to gather the lost sheep of Israel in loving kindness (see Matthew 10:5), He journeys through Samaria and shares the gospel first with the Samaritan woman drawing water at the well of Jacob. He then shares the gospel with many other Samaritans.

CONCLUSION

These are but a few of the Jewish-Samaritan interactions that we encounter in the pages of the New Testament. As we come across additional references, our new understanding of the way that the Jews and Samaritans viewed themselves and each other can offer us additional insights to the social context that gives life to the scriptures. As we listen to those different stories, perhaps we are then practicing one form of neighborliness: understanding the perspectives of others from their own viewpoint.

MATTHEW 18 AND LUKE 10: WHAT IS THE KINGDOM OF GOD?

"AND WHO IS MY NEIGHBOR?"

This is the great question of the good Samaritan story, a story we have all listened to carefully many times as we have studied the different characters, the plot line, and ultimately the loving compassion and mercy that one human shared with another. When we view this timeless question from the perspective of it its surrounding context, the richness of Christ's message is enhanced.

The stories and passages surrounding the good Samaritan story in Luke 10 are focused on building the kingdom of God through preaching the gospel and gathering souls. In this context, the Good Samaritan story is more than just a parable about being neighborly or showing loving compassion. It is a parable about the kingdom of God, or at least the type of individual who is invited into the kingdom of God. Similarly, Matthew 18 is a chapter that focuses on the conditions that mark the kingdom of God and the characteristics of those who comprise that kingdom.

Let's now look at those chapters again—not so much as to focus on the beautiful and well-known story of the good Samaritan, but rather to understand the conditions of the kingdom of God (see Matthew 18) and the gospel call for us to be gathered in unto God (see Luke 10). We'll explore these various passages in a commentary style, clarifying them with other scriptures and ancient languages.

MATTHEW 18—CHARACTERISTICS AND CONDITIONS OF THE KINGDOM OF GOD

Those in the Kingdom of God are Like Little Children—Matthew 18:1–6

As Matthew chapter 18 opens, we find Christ's disciples wondering who will be the greatest in the kingdom of heaven. Apparently this was a persisting question among them, for we find a similar episode on the night before Christ's suffering when they had gathered to partake of the Passover meal:

> And there was also a strife among them, which of them should be accounted the greatest.
>
> And he said unto them, The kings of the Gentiles exercise lordship over them; and they that exercise authority upon them are called benefactors.
>
> But ye *shall* not *be* so: but he that is greatest among you, let him be as the younger; and he that is chief, as he that doth serve.
>
> For whether *is* greater, he that sitteth at meat, or he that serveth? *is* not he that sitteth at meat? but I am among you as he that serveth.
>
> Ye are they which have continued with me in my temptations.
>
> And I appoint unto you a kingdom, as my Father hath appointed unto me;
>
> That ye may eat and drink at my table in my kingdom, and sit on thrones judging the twelve tribes of Israel. (Luke 22:24–30)

In the days of Christ, social boundaries were especially clearly marked and on display when meals were served. The guests were arranged according to their social station. Those of the greatest social stature were placed closest to the patron of the home; those of lesser rank and prestige were placed farther away. Those who served the meal had no social standing. This eating arrangement—which most likely imitated royal banquet patterns, where political figures were placed at the banquet table in relation to the king based on their relative authority—created a visual display that left no one in doubt of a person's relative "greatness" in the social order.[24]

---

[24] See the following studies for more information about the culture of food and meals

Apparently, the disciples of Christ misunderstood the true meaning of *the kingdom of heaven*. They argued about who would be the greatest among them and who would sit closest to Christ at the meal. So Christ taught them that true power and greatness is found in humility and service.

Returning to Matthew 18, we find a similar teaching from Christ to His disciples when they disputed over greatness. He placed a child in their midst and offered them the promise that whoever would be like a child would be greatest in the kingdom of heaven: "He that shall humble himself shall be exalted" (Matthew 23:12).

This message is also found in the Book of Mormon. Upon transferring the Nephite kingdom to his son Mosiah, King Benjamin gathered his people together that he might share with them the gospel message and his witness of Jesus Christ. In context, however, his speech also served as an exhortation to live according to a higher social and political order that peace might reign throughout the Nephite kingdom. With loving tenderness, King Benjamin reminded his people that only those who are childlike inherit the true kingdom: "For the natural man is an enemy to God, and has been from the fall of Adam, and will be, forever and ever, unless he yields to the enticings of the Holy Spirit, and putteth off the natural man and becometh a saint through the atonement of Christ the Lord, and becometh as a child, submissive, meek, humble, patient, full of love, willing to submit to all things which the Lord seeth fit to inflict upon him, even as a child doth submit to his father" (Mosiah 3:19).

Unity Prevails in the Kingdom of God—Matthew 18:7–14

This next passage explores the unity that prevails in the kingdom of God. Some may read Matthew 18:8–9 quite literally and suppose that they should chop off their hand if they ever steal or pluck out their eye if they ever see anything unholy. However, Christ was not referring to the literal parts of our body, but rather to the "body of saints." The JST of Matthew 18:9 helps to clarify this concept: "And a man's hand is his friend, and his foot, also; and a man's eye, are they of his own household."

---

in ancient Mediterranean society: Peter Garnsey, *Food and Society in Classical Antiquity* (Cambridge: Cambridge University Press, 1999); Inge Nielsen and Hanne Sigismund Nielsen, eds., *Meals in a Social Context: Aspects of the Communal Meal in the Hellenistic and Roman World* (Oxford: Aarhus University Press, 1998).

Paul, the ancient Apostle, also spoke of a similar concept when writing to the Roman saints. Apparently, the Christians at Rome had struggled with division and controversy in their congregation. Perhaps they even struggled, as had Christ's disciples, with the question of who was greatest in the kingdom of God. So Paul wrote to remind them that they were to be a unified whole, a single body, yet differing in abilities, gifts, and offices:

> I beseech you therefore, brethren, by the mercies of God, that ye present your bodies a living sacrifice, holy, acceptable unto God, which is your reasonable service.
>
> And be not conformed to this world: but be ye transformed by the renewing of your mind, that ye may prove what is that good, and acceptable, and perfect, will of God.
>
> For I say, through the grace given unto me, to every man that is among you, not to think of himself more highly than he ought to think; but to think soberly, according as God hath dealt to every man the measure of faith.
>
> For as we have many members in one body, and all members have not the same office:
>
> So we, being many, are one body in Christ, and every one members one of another. (Romans 12:1–5)

For the sake of comparison, an alternative translation of the same passage is in the New Revised Standard Version (NRSV):[25]

> I appeal to you therefore, brothers and sisters, by the mercies of God, to present your bodies as a living sacrifice, holy and acceptable to God, which is your spiritual worship.
>
> Do not be conformed to this world, but be transformed by the renewing of your minds, so that you may discern what is the will of God--what is good and acceptable and perfect.
>
> For by the grace given to me I say to everyone among you not to think of yourself more highly than you ought to think, but

---

[25] *The New Revised Standard Version (NRSV) of the Bible*, copyrighted 1989 by the Division of Christian Education of the National Council of the Churches of Christ in the United States of America.

to think with sober judgment, each according to the measure of faith that God has assigned.

For as in one body we have many members, and not all the members have the same function,

so we, who are many, are one body in Christ, and individually we are members one of another.

THE KINGDOM OF GOD IS HOLY—MATTHEW 18:15–20

It is not enough, however, for the kingdom of God to be unified; it must also be holy. Thus the body of Saints must likewise be holy. Each person must individually be clean and pure; if not, he or she will be cut off from the body so as not to pollute the entire body.

What we first notice in these verses is that Christ establishes a forum for dealing with offenses and difficulties within the Christian community (in other words, within the kingdom of God on earth) that threaten its sanctity and holiness. In verses 15–17, Christ explains that private trespasses are to be dealt with privately while public trespasses are to be dealt with publicly, as long as there are witnesses.

We find an example of this in the New Testament where Paul attempted to rid the body of polluted and impenitent members according to the law of witnesses that the kingdom of God might not be corrupted by any form of impurity:

It is reported commonly that there is fornication among you, and such fornication as is not so much as named among the Gentiles, that one should have his father's wife.

And ye are puffed up, and have not rather mourned, that he that hath done this deed might be taken away from among you.

For I verily, as absent in body, but present in spirit, have judged already, as though I were present, concerning him that hath so done this deed,

In the name of our Lord Jesus Christ, when ye are gathered together, and my spirit, with the power of our Lord Jesus Christ,

To deliver such an one unto Satan for the destruction of the flesh, that the spirit may be saved in the day of the Lord Jesus.

Your glorying is not good. Know ye not that a little leaven leaveneth the whole lump?

Purge out therefore the old leaven, that ye may be a new lump, as ye are unleavened. For even Christ our passover is sacrificed for us:

Therefore let us keep the feast, not with old leaven, neither with the leaven of malice and wickedness; but with the unleavened bread of sincerity and truth.

I wrote unto you in an epistle not to company with fornicators:

Yet not altogether with the fornicators of this world, or with the covetous, or extortioners, or with idolaters; for then must ye needs go out of the world.

But now I have written unto you not to keep company, if any man that is called a brother be a fornicator, or covetous, or an idolater, or a railer, or a drunkard, or an extortioner; with such an one no not to eat.

For what have I to do to judge them also that are without? do not ye judge them that are within?

But them that are without God judgeth. Therefore put away from among yourselves that wicked person. (1 Corinthians 5:1–13)

The NRSV translates this passage as:

It is actually reported that there is sexual immorality among you, and of a kind that is not found even among pagans; for a man is living with his father's wife.

And you are arrogant! Should you not rather have mourned, so that he who has done this would have been removed from among you?

For though absent in body, I am present in spirit; and as if present I have already pronounced judgment

in the name of the Lord Jesus on the man who has done such a thing. When you are assembled, and my spirit is present with the power of our Lord Jesus,

you are to hand this man over to Satan for the destruction of the flesh, so that his spirit may be saved in the day of the Lord.

Your boasting is not a good thing. Do you not know that a little yeast leavens the whole batch of dough?

Clean out the old yeast so that you may be a new batch, as you really are unleavened. For our paschal lamb, Christ, has been sacrificed.

Therefore, let us celebrate the festival, not with the old yeast, the yeast of malice and evil, but with the unleavened bread of sincerity and truth.

I wrote to you in my letter not to associate with sexually immoral persons—

not at all meaning the immoral of this world, or the greedy and robbers, or idolaters, since you would then need to go out of the world.

But now I am writing to you not to associate with anyone who bears the name of brother or sister who is sexually immoral or greedy, or is an idolater, reviler, drunkard, or robber. Do not even eat with such a one.

For what have I to do with judging those outside? Is it not those who are inside that you are to judge?

God will judge those outside. "Drive out the wicked person from among you."

Returning to Christ's message in Matthew 18 concerning regulations for the kingdom of God, he goes on to say that whosoever in the kingdom will not abide by the standards of the kingdom (in other words, the Church) should be "unto thee as an heathen and a publican" (Matthew 18:17). What does this mean? Christ is saying that if one desires to be part of the kingdom of God but refuses to resolve his or her offenses and difficulties by the standards of the Christian community, then the kingdom of God serves no purpose for that individual. It would be better for that individual to remain among the non-Christian communities (in other words, the heathen and pagan communities). In his exhortations to the Corinthian Christians to establish the conditions of the kingdom of God on earth, Paul stresses the idea that difficulties and conflicts among the Christians should be resolved within the community itself instead of taking the "dirty laundry" before unholy heathen judges:

Dare any of you, having a matter against another, go to law before the unjust, and not before the saints?

Do ye not know that the saints shall judge the world? and if the world shall be judged by you, are ye unworthy to judge the smallest matters?

Know ye not that we shall judge angels? how much more things that pertain to this life? If then ye have judgments of things pertaining to this life, set them to judge who are least esteemed in the church.

I speak to your shame. Is it so, that there is not a wise man among you? no, not one that shall be able to judge between his brethren?

But brother goeth to law with brother, and that before the unbelievers.

Now therefore there is utterly a fault among you, because ye go to law one with another. Why do ye not rather take wrong? why do ye not rather suffer yourselves to be defrauded?

Nay, ye do wrong, and defraud, and that *your* brethren.

Know ye not that the unrighteous shall not inherit the kingdom of God? Be not deceived: neither fornicators, nor idolaters, nor adulterers, nor effeminate, nor abusers of themselves with mankind,

Nor thieves, nor covetous, nor drunkards, nor revilers, nor extortioners, shall inherit the kingdom of God.

And such were some of you: but ye are washed, but ye are sanctified, but ye are justified in the name of the Lord Jesus, and by the Spirit of our God. (1 Corinthians 6:1–11)

The NRSV translates this passage as:

When any of you has a grievance against another, do you dare to take it to court before the unrighteous, instead of taking it before the saints?

Do you not know that the saints will judge the world? And if the world is to be judged by you, are you incompetent to try trivial cases?

Do you not know that we are to judge angels-- to say nothing of ordinary matters?

If you have ordinary cases, then, do you appoint as judges those who have no standing in the church?

I say this to your shame. Can it be that there is no one among you wise enough to decide between one believer and another,

but a believer goes to court against a believer-- and before unbelievers at that?

In fact, to have lawsuits at all with one another is already a defeat for you. Why not rather be wronged? Why not rather be defrauded?

But you yourselves wrong and defraud-- and believers at that.

Do you not know that wrongdoers will not inherit the kingdom of God? Do not be deceived! Fornicators, idolaters, adulterers, male prostitutes, sodomites,

thieves, the greedy, drunkards, revilers, robbers-- none of these will inherit the kingdom of God.

And this is what some of you used to be. But you were washed, you were sanctified, you were justified in the name of the Lord Jesus Christ and in the Spirit of our God.

Christ continues His message in Matthew 18:18–20, explaining that all things in the kingdom of God are to be regulated according to the power of the priesthood, with Christ at the center. This is the meaning of "there am I in the midst of them" (Matthew 18:20). The word *midst* refers to the very center or to the focal point. If the members do not have Christ at the center of their judgments and relationships, then truly they are as the heathen and publicans that are without Christ.

THE MERCIFUL INHERIT THE KINGDOM OF GOD—
MATTHEW 18:21–35

This passage begins with a query from inquisitive Peter, who desired to know his responsibilities to forgive others. He asked if he was required to forgive seven times; the Lord responds, nay, but "seventy times seven" (Matthew 18:22).

Obviously, we are not to interpret this literally—that we are to forgive seven times only or four hundred and ninety times only. These numbers were symbolic and expressive. The number seven, in Jewish understanding, represented perfection, fullness and completion, while four hundred and ninety is a forceful intensification of this perfection. It is also interesting to note that the Hebrew word for "seven" and "covenant" both come from the same word: *sheva*.

In essence, Peter is asking if he is to forgive fully and completely. Christ affirms this, while significantly intensifying the responsibility to *always* perfectly, fully, and completely forgive, as symbolized by four hundred and ninety times.

Perhaps one of the most challenging things in life is to forgive fully, perfectly, and completely, even if those who have harmed us continue to believe that their actions were justified and thus show no remorse nor restitution. If we do not forgive, however, we cannot experience the purity of joy that God has designed for us, nor can we receive forgiveness of our own sins: "For if ye forgive men their trespasses, your heavenly Father will also forgive you: But if ye forgive not men their trespasses, neither will your Father forgive your trespasses" (Matthew 6:14–15).

To illustrate this teaching about forgiveness, Christ relates to His disciples a parable of a kingdom. In this parable, a servant who is in extraordinary debt to the king begs forgiveness. Showing unparalleled compassion, the king freely forgives the servant. However, this same servant later finds his fellow servant who is in debt to him and demands immediate payment. When the fellow servant cannot pay, the recently forgiven servant exercises unrighteous dominion and has the man incarcerated. For this grievous assault on justice and mercy, the king takes the unforgiving servant and delivers him to the tormentors—or, literally, "the torturers." This wicked servant was to be tortured until he could pay off his debt in full. And since he had no way of paying off that debt in full (and never would so long as he was under the power of the torturers), this could lead to the interpretation that the servant would be tormented indefinitely.

In monetary terms, this story is all the more remarkable when we realize that the unforgiving servant owed the king nearly $37 billion, while his fellow servant owed the measly sum of $10,000. The wicked servant's debt was 3.7 million times greater than that of his fellow servant. Truly the principle that "where much is given much is required" even applies to compassion, mercy, and forgiveness. If we hope to qualify for the kingdom of God, we must exercise mercy as did the exemplary king of this parable.

LUKE 10—GATHERING INTO THE KINGDOM OF GOD

We reviewed in Matthew 18 various characteristics and conditions of the kingdom of God and those who inhabit it. But the kingdom is empty until souls are gathered into it. Luke 10 is a chapter of gathering, and with this lens let's view the passages of this chapter.

CALLING AND EMPOWERING THE HARVESTERS—LUKE 10:1-16

The harvest was great and the laborers were few. So Christ called additional disciples to labor with him in gathering souls into the kingdom of God. Before sending them on their assigned missions, He gave them instructions fit for the preaching circumstances of their day and time. He also gave them power to heal the sick. This is a sign of the kingdom of God on earth, which is a kingdom of healing and wholeness. It is interesting to note how some of the New Testament healing miracles come in the context of kingdom of God passages.

Unfortunately, not all people will hearken to the call to gather unto God. Christ expressed that lamentation with utterances of woe on impenitent Jewish cities such as Chorazin, Bethsaida, and Capernaum. He compared them to the gentile cities of Tyre and Sidon, whose inhabitants would readily accept the kingdom of God if preached to, even though they were not of the elect. This is reminiscent of what we hear in the Book of Mormon when Alma and Amulek called the wicked people of Ammonihah to repentance:

> Behold, do ye not remember the words which he spake unto Lehi, saying that: Inasmuch as ye shall keep my commandments, ye shall prosper in the land? And again it is said that: Inasmuch as ye will not keep my commandments ye shall be cut off from the presence of the Lord.
>
> Now I would that ye should remember, that inasmuch as the Lamanites have not kept the commandments of God, they have been cut off from the presence of the Lord. Now we see that the word of the Lord has been verified in this thing, and the Lamanites have been cut off from his presence, from the beginning of their transgressions in the land.
>
> Nevertheless I say unto you, that it shall be more tolerable for them in the day of judgment than for you, if ye remain in your sins, yea, and even more tolerable for them in this life than for you, except ye repent. (Alma 9:13–15)

PRIESTHOOD POWER ENTRUSTED TO THE GATHERERS—
LUKE 10:17–20

When the disciples returned from their appointed missions, they rejoiced in the success they had found. Christ then blessed each of them with additional priesthood power over the forces of the adversary—forces that are symbolized by serpents and scorpions. This harks back to the Garden of Eden story where Adam is given power to crush the head of the serpent (see Genesis 3:15). In terms of priesthood power, this refers to the ability to overcome Satan and his evil work.

Additionally, Christ draws on another Old Testament theme, this time from Isaiah, to paint the cosmic drama in which Satan was overpowered by the forces of God and cast out of heaven (see Isaiah 14:12–27). With the endowment of priesthood power, then, the gatherers are prepared to cast out the prince of this world that it might be prepared for the kingdom of God.

THE KINGDOM OF GOD IS REVEALED TO THE CHILDLIKE—
LUKE 10:21–24

What we learn in these verses is that the kingdom of God had long been in anticipation among prophets, priests, and kings. Yet it is only the humble, the meek, and the childlike who are given to see the establishment of God's kingdom on earth. This is the same message that Christ shared not many years later with the Nephite faithful in the New World:

> Behold, I am Jesus Christ the Son of God. I created the heavens and the earth, and all things that in them are. I was with the Father from the beginning. I am in the Father, and the Father in me; and in me hath the Father glorified his name.
>
> I came unto my own, and my own received me not. And the scriptures concerning my coming are fulfilled.
>
> And as many as have received me, to them have I given to become the sons of God; and even so will I to as many as shall believe on my name, for behold, by me redemption cometh, and in me is the law of Moses fulfilled.
>
> I am the light and the life of the world. I am Alpha and Omega, the beginning and the end.

And ye shall offer up unto me no more the shedding of blood; yea, your sacrifices and your burnt offerings shall be done away, for I will accept none of your sacrifices and your burnt offerings.

And ye shall offer for a sacrifice unto me a broken heart and a contrite spirit. And whoso cometh unto me with a broken heart and a contrite spirit, him will I baptize with fire and with the Holy Ghost, even as the Lamanites, because of their faith in me at the time of their conversion, were baptized with fire and with the Holy Ghost, and they knew it not.

Behold, I have come unto the world to bring redemption unto the world, to save the world from sin.

Therefore, whoso repenteth and cometh unto me as a little child, him will I receive, for of such is the kingdom of God. Behold, for such I have laid down my life, and have taken it up again; therefore repent, and come unto me ye ends of the earth, and be saved. (3 Nephi 9:15–22; emphasis added)

THE KINGDOM OF GOD IS FOR GOOD NEIGHBORS— LUKE 10:25–37

This is a beautiful and well-known story of the most unlikely of characters offering loving compassion to another. In the story, the Samaritan pours wine and oil into the wounds of the broken man. The way Jews named "wine" and "oil" in Hebrew adds tremendous significance to the story: wine is often called "blood of grapes," and oil is called "blood of olives." Since blood is a symbol of life, the good Samaritan symbolically poured new life into a man who was half dead.

When we read this story not just as an invitation to be neighborly to all but as a representative example of the type of individuals who are invited into the kingdom of God, the story takes on new meaning. In other words, the powerful messages expressed in Matthew 18 and Luke 10 concerning the kingdom of God can serve as lens through which we now can view the good Samaritan story with new eyes. Hence, in the context of the kingdom of God passages we have explored thus far, the significance of the good Samaritan story becomes very rich indeed. Notice the luxuriant tapestry of scriptural connections between the good Samaritan story and Old Testament scriptures such as Deuteronomy 6:4–5 and Leviticus 19:18, 34.

DUTIES IN THE KINGDOM OF GOD—LUKE 10:38-42

In this final passage of the chapter, we find Christ at the home of Mary and Martha. Mary sat at Jesus's feet hearing Him teach the words of eternal life, while Martha busied herself with the duties of hospitality that were ever so important in that culture. Martha was frustrated that Mary did not aid her in these duties. Christ used the opportunity to teach a powerful lesson about the kingdom of God when He turned to Martha and said, "Martha, Martha, thou art careful and troubled about many things: But one thing is needful: and Mary hath chosen that good part, which shall not be taken away from her" (Luke 10:41–42).

Let's to look at alternate meanings of a few of the underlying Greek words of this passage. Christ states that Martha is *troubled*. An alternate translation would say that she was "distracted." Christ also states that "one thing is needful." The underlying Greek for *needful* could also be translated as "duty or task." Clearly Christ is teaching that we should not let important things, even the culturally important need to be hospitable, distract us from the most important things, which are the duties of the kingdom of God. Mary had chosen the better part: the duty to be with the living Lord who delivers the Living Word.

CONCLUSION

The scriptures are rich and inexhaustible in meaning and application. As we press forward in the duty to search the living words of Christ, our personal burdens will appear lighter as we are strengthened through the Spirit of God, and our souls will be empowered to live according to the laws of the kingdom of God. We will find our hearts purified, our joy will be full, and we will be, as it were, little children in the presence of our God. Then we shall see the kingdom of God and inherit the everlasting joys of that kingdom prepared for those who faithfully endure until the end.

LUKE 15 AND 17: LOST AND FOUND

"The kingdom of God is within you."
—*Luke 17:21*

SOME OF THE MOST NOURISHING and healing stories that span all cultures are those that speak of wandering souls finding their way home, the hero discovering his true identity, and the royal celebration at finding the kingdom. All of these pertain to finding that which was lost, as does the scriptural pearl in Luke 17:21: "The kingdom of God is within you."

This deceptively simple statement is full of marvelous truths. Consider that each of us is on the mortal journey, seeking with great diligence to find the kingdom of God, to return home from whence we came. We are as lost strangers, sojourners in the wilderness, "our lives passed away like as it were unto us a dream, we being a lonesome and a solemn people, wanderers, cast out" (Jacob 7:26).

In reality, though, we are not lost—not cast out from the kingdom of God. Indeed, as we learn in the Gospel of Luke, the kingdom of God is among us, around us, and within us. We *are* home, for God is with us; we simply need to recognize Him in our lives and let the power of His kingdom live through us. When we realize that the kingdom of God is within us, we are then no longer lost, but are found.

What does it require to discover the kingdom of God within us? The fiery spark of the Holy Spirit can awaken our ancient soul and draw it out to our Everlasting Father and Maker. Like a royal cloak, His love will gently descend on us, and we will be bound to Him through eternal and unbreakable bonds. He ever seeks us, more fervently than we desire to find Him or to be found.

Sometimes we are so overwhelmed with the feeling that we are lost and so far from home that we fail to see the divine within us placed there by God like a signet ring testifying that we truly are members of his royal household. When our souls awaken to these truths, we then recognize ourselves and we know ourselves truly: the hero who has braved the fiery depths to overcome all through faith. We are most real, most alive, most happy, and most full of joy when we have discovered our true identity. That true hero identity is within us, intimately bound up to the kingdom of God within.

Several New Testament chapters contain stories and parables that pertain to finding the kingdom of God and the conditions of that kingdom. The principles in these stories and parables can enlighten our understanding of the kingdom of God and guide us to discover it within ourselves.

PARABLE OF THE LOST SHEEP (LUKE 15:3–7)

This kingdom of God parable revolves around the great joy that is to be had when the lost soul is found. We may liken this scripture unto ourselves by considering that in our own lives the Lord plays the role of searching for us in the most foreboding wilderness. He will not give up the search until He has found us, and then there will be great rejoicing.

PARABLE OF THE LOST COIN (LUKE 15:8–10)

This parable is along the same idea as the parable of the lost sheep; this parable also focuses on the great joy that occurs when a precious lost treasure is recovered. This parable also provides insight into one of the ways we might discover our true selves and the kingdom of God within us—repentance!

PARABLE OF THE PRODIGAL SON (LUKE 15:11–32)

While somewhat longer and more complex, this parable follows a pattern similar to that of great hero stories. The hero (though admittedly in this case the main character acts more like swine than a prince) leaves his father's home, sure of his identity and secure in his inheritance. He enters the great city (the world) and engages in riotous living. During that process, the royal image within him is dimmed and eventually forgotten.

In the darkest moment, the Spirit awakens within the hero the knowledge of his true identity and the royal lineage that is his. He begins to recognize the kingdom of God within him; as he embraces that reality, he leaves behind the swine and grime of the world.

Like the woman who found the precious treasure, like the man who discovered the beloved sheep wandering in the lone and dreary wilderness, great rejoicing erupts when the son is once again safely home. The father initiates this outpouring of joy on behalf of the son who has discovered his true identity and returned home.

This is both a great hero story and a great healing story. We learn that no matter how far we have strayed from home, no matter how dark our forgetfulness of the kingdom that lives within us, we can be reclaimed through God's grace and once again be granted the beloved title of son or daughter.

THE DUTIES OF MEMBERS OF THE KINGDOM (LUKE 17:3–10)

Lest we think the divine spark that enlightens and enlivens us is a passport to a life without spiritual responsibilities, Jesus shares several short pieces of wisdom in Luke 17:3–10. Jesus originally delivered these to His disciples to encourage them to remember their duties to forgive their brethren, an important element of repentance both for the sinner and the afflicted. Jesus underscores the importance of forgiveness by reminding His disciples that they are chosen servants in the kingdom of God—and as servants they are expected to obey if they desire the promised blessings. Apparently the disciples needed this encouragement as they pled with the Lord to increase their courage and faith so they could live as He had taught them.

HEALING AND CLEANSING IN THE KINGDOM OF GOD (LUKE 17:11–21)

Earlier we had a parable of ten precious coins; one of the ten was lost and then found. The ten lepers story here follows a similar format. In many ways, we are like lepers overcome with the diseases of a fallen world. We learn from the stranger in this passage, even a lowly Samaritan, that we must never forget who has bought us, who has saved us, and what price was offered that we might no longer be strangers but fellow citizens in the kingdom of God. Christ will cleanse us and our faith will make us whole.

EVER SEEKING BUT NEVER COMING TO A KNOWLEDGE OF THE TRUTH (LUKE 17:20–21)

In this episode, the Pharisees come to Jesus seeking sure knowledge of the coming of the kingdom of God. However, the Pharisees failed to recognize, and Christ was quick to point out, that the kingdom would not be revealed as some glorious manifestation. Instead, it was evident in each of those who exercised faith unto repentance, living lives of committed servants to the Heavenly King. The kingdom was to be found through the quiet introspection of contrition.

THE LAST DAYS AND THE COMING KING (LUKE 17:22–37)

Christ instructed His disciples on signs of the times for His expected coming. He had already taught them to find the kingdom of God within, but they also needed to understand how to navigate the events that occurred around them so they would not be deceived. Those who have come to fully recognize their true selves through the revelatory power of God's Spirit will not be deceived. They will stand in holy places and be gathered in with the Saints while the world continues to wallow in darkness and confusion.

GOD'S OWN KINGDOM

God knows His people. Do we know ourselves? Do we recognize who we are? Have we let the Spirit search our hearts and reveal the stunning truth of our origin and divine possibilities? Or do we presently feel lost? Do we believe in the reality of the at-one-ment, that great power to bring all truth into one great whole, uniting and binding the souls of the righteous to God?

We can be reclaimed. We can be found. We can be recognized by God and by ourselves, our true selves. Let us open our hearts and discover ourselves as we discover Him.

MATTHEW 25: PREPARING FOR THE KINGDOM OF HEAVEN

IMAGINE WALKING INTO A PACKED theater just when the show is most dramatic and exciting. All the moviegoers are sitting on the edge of their seats, ears attuned to every uttered word lest they miss something of great importance. The intensity of the moment is palpable. But you missed everything that went before, so you have no clue as to why this moment is of such import and intensity. Even though you're clueless about the whole thing you dare not interrupt anyone to find out what led up to this moment. You don't want to cause anyone to miss the climax!

Fortunately, we're not walking into a live performance as Matthew 25 begins. We have the benefit of being able to review what went on before (Matthew 24) so we can understand the full intensity of the immensely relevant parables and exhortations of Matthew 25. If we stepped into Matthew 25 without the requisite preparation of Matthew 24, we certainly would feel the palpable intensity and urgency of the Lord's message without fully understanding why.

Using parables as a method for teaching the truth, Matthew 25 covers several key themes of the gospel: the kingdom of God, seeking the kingdom of God, preparing for the kingdom of God, and inheriting the kingdom of God.

Because Matthew 25 is a continuation of Christ's preaching of the coming kingdom of Heaven found in Matthew 24 (also found in Joseph Smith—Matthew in the Pearl of Great Price), let's briefly review the "first act" in Matthew 24 so the Matthew 25 parables will resound with greater intensity and importance.

JOSEPH SMITH MATTHEW 24—THE DAY OF THE LORD

A personal note seems important here. The topic of the day of the Lord (found throughout Matthew 24 and 25) can easily lead to doomsday discussions and feelings of hopelessness or despair—something that might be particularly so in light of the swirling confusion of current world events. I personally do not believe that the Lord spoke these words to whip us into a frenzy of doomsday despair. Instead, remember that "Adam fell that men might be; and men are, that they might have *joy*" (2 Nephi 2:25; emphasis added). Though pain, trial, tribulation, and even mighty destructions will take place, the Lord does not speak of these things to our despair, unless we need to repent (see Mormon 10:22), but rather that we might understand and be saved.

Being a people who believe in continuing revelation, we can use the Joseph Smith Translation) of Matthew 24 in the Pearl of Great Price (see pages 43–46 of the 1981 English edition). The chapter begins with an introductory statement that shapes the discussion throughout; in it, Christ reveals to His disciples that He will again come to earth. Newly enlightened, the disciples ask, "Tell us when shall these things be which thou has said concerning the destruction of the temple, and the Jews; and what is the sign of thy coming, and of the end of the world, or the destruction of the wicked, which is the end of the world?" (JS–Matthew 24:5).

In response, Christ describes how wickedness will abound among the Jews and other nations, how the disciples will be killed, how false prophets and false Christs will arise, and how the Jewish temple and nation will be destroyed.

Christ then shifts focus from the destruction and calamities of ancient days to the perplexities and commotion of the latter days. He reveals the signs of His coming and describes some of the tribulations and destructions that will happen throughout the earth at that time.

Christ cautions His disciples to be wise and to not be deceived. Several parables underscore this caution: those who know the signs of His coming and, more importantly, live righteously will not be deceived and thus will have no need of fear or concern. He then exhorts His disciples, again by means of a parable, to not despair and think that He has delayed His coming, for He will come, just as surely as the sun rises to greet the new day.

It is here that the intense expectation of the coming of the Lord reaches its height. We are about to hear a full description of that day, but the chapter ends. Going back to the movie or play analogy, many leave during this intermission and fail to return for the second act. However, all you have to do is turn to Matthew 25 to hear the rest of the Lord's oration on this subject.

MATTHEW 25—THE COMING OF THE KINGDOM OF HEAVEN

Matthew 25 is the second (and often neglected) half of Christ's two-part sermon regarding the destruction of the Jewish nation and His eventual triumphal return in the last days. This chapter is a series of three well-known parables: the parable of the ten virgins, the parable of the talents, and the parable of the goats and the sheep. But since Matthew 25 is seldom read in context of Matthew 24, most of us miss the real significance and power of these unique parables.

Each of these parables teaches us what types of individuals will be found on the earth when the Lord returns. On the one hand will be those prepared to receive the invitation into the kingdom of Heaven. On the other hand will be those who knew not the Lord and hence were not known by Him. By searching Matthew 25 diligently, we find the doctrines and truths that can spiritually prepare us for the coming kingdom heralded by the returning Lord Himself.

THE PARABLE OF THE TEN VIRGINS (MATTHEW 25:1–13)

This parable presents both a scene and a problem. Ten virgins are waiting for the bridegroom; the five who were wise were truly prepared for the coming celebrant, but the five who were foolish were not. It is obvious to our gospel-trained eyes that the bridegroom is none other than Jesus Christ. He brings with Him the wedding party; His entourage is the kingdom of Heaven. As the kingdom advances to the wedding feast, which is none other than the feast of the sacramental table, guests continue to join the thronging multitude. There is great joy and anticipation of the mighty celebration and outpouring of rejoicing that will take place at the wedding feast.

Several Old Testament writers took up the idea of the coming bridegroom. A close study of those relevant passages reveals a number of relevant themes: The bridegroom brings with him the promise of safety, security, renewal, increase, and all of the blessings of happiness, restoration, and enduring life. Those powerful themes are particularly shown in a few Old Testament passages: one comes from the poetic book of Psalms, two passages were penned by the visionary Isaiah, and the final passage was uttered by Jeremiah, who witnessed the destruction of Jerusalem. I've added bold emphasis to the word **bridegroom** in these passages.

Psalms 19:1–10

The heavens declare the glory of God; and the firmament sheweth his handywork.

Day unto day uttereth speech, and night unto night sheweth knowledge.

There is no speech nor language, where their voice is not heard.

Their line is gone out through all the earth, and their words to the end of the world. In them hath he set a tabernacle for the sun,

Which is as a **bridegroom** coming out of his chamber, and rejoiceth as a strong man to run a race.

His going forth *is* from the end of the heaven, and his circuit unto the ends of it: and there is nothing hid from the heat thereof.

The law of the LORD *is* perfect, converting the soul: the testimony of the LORD is sure, making wise the simple.

The statutes of the LORD are right, rejoicing the heart: the commandment of the LORD is pure, enlightening the eyes.

The fear of the LORD is clean, enduring for ever: the judgments of the LORD are true and righteous altogether.

More to be desired are they than gold, yea, than much fine gold: sweeter also than honey and the honeycomb.

Isaiah 61:1–11 (Jesus quotes from this text when He announced His mission at the synagogue of Nazareth)

The Spirit of the Lord GOD is upon me; because the LORD hath anointed me to preach good tidings unto the meek; he hath sent me to bind up the brokenhearted, to proclaim liberty to the captives, and the opening of the prison to them that are bound;

To proclaim the acceptable year of the LORD, and the day of vengeance of our God; to comfort all that mourn;

To appoint unto them that mourn in Zion, to give unto them beauty for ashes, the oil of joy for mourning, the garment of praise for the spirit of heaviness; that they might be called trees of righteousness, the planting of the LORD, that he might be glorified.

And they shall build the old wastes, they shall raise up the former desolations, and they shall repair the waste cities, the desolations of many generations.

And strangers shall stand and feed your flocks, and the sons of the alien shall be your plowmen and your vinedressers.

But ye shall be named the Priests of the LORD: men shall call you the Ministers of our God: ye shall eat the riches of the Gentiles, and in their glory shall ye boast yourselves.

For your shame ye shall have double; and for confusion they shall rejoice in their portion: therefore in their land they shall possess the double: everlasting joy shall be unto them.

For I the LORD love judgment, I hate robbery for burnt offering; and I will direct their work in truth, and I will make an everlasting covenant with them.

And their seed shall be known among the Gentiles, and their offspring among the people: all that see them shall acknowledge them, that they are the seed which the LORD hath blessed.

I will greatly rejoice in the LORD, my soul shall be joyful in my God; for he hath clothed me with the garments of salvation, he hath covered me with the robe of righteousness, as a **bridegroom** decketh himself with ornaments, and as a bride adorneth herself with her jewels.

For as the earth bringeth forth her bud, and as the garden causeth the things that are sown in it to spring forth; so the Lord GOD will cause righteousness and praise to spring forth before all the nations.

Isaiah 62:1–12

For Zion's sake will I not hold my peace, and for Jerusalem's sake I will not rest, until the righteousness thereof go forth as brightness, and the salvation thereof as a lamp that burneth.

And the Gentiles shall see thy righteousness, and all kings thy glory: and thou shalt be called by a new name, which the mouth of the LORD shall name.

Thou shalt also be a crown of glory in the hand of the LORD, and a royal diadem in the hand of thy God.

Thou shalt no more be termed Forsaken; neither shall thy land any more be termed Desolate: but thou shalt be called Hephzi-bah, and thy land Beulah: for the LORD delighteth in thee, and thy land shall be married.

For as a young man marrieth a virgin, so shall thy sons marry thee: and as the **bridegroom** rejoiceth over the bride, so shall thy God rejoice over thee.

I have set watchmen upon thy walls, O Jerusalem, which shall never hold their peace day nor night: ye that make mention of the LORD, keep not silence,

And give him no rest, till he establish, and till he make Jerusalem a praise in the earth.

The LORD hath sworn by his right hand, and by the arm of his strength, Surely I will no more give thy corn to be meat for thine enemies; and the sons of the stranger shall not drink thy wine, for the which thou hast laboured:

But they that have gathered it shall eat it, and praise the LORD; and they that have brought it together shall drink it in the courts of my holiness.

Go through, go through the gates; prepare ye the way of the people; cast up, cast up the highway; gather out the stones; lift up a standard for the people.

Behold, the LORD hath proclaimed unto the end of the world, Say ye to the daughter of Zion, Behold, thy salvation cometh; behold, his reward is with him, and his work before him.

And they shall call them, The holy people, The redeemed of the LORD: and thou shalt be called, Sought out, A city not forsaken.

Jeremiah 33:9–14

And it shall be to me a name of joy, a praise and an honour before all the nations of the earth, which shall hear all the good that I do unto them: and they shall fear and tremble for all the goodness and for all the prosperity that I procure unto it.

Thus saith the LORD; Again there shall be heard in this place, which ye say shall be desolate without man and without beast, even in the cities of Judah, and in the streets of Jerusalem, that are desolate, without man, and without inhabitant, and without beast,

The voice of joy, and the voice of gladness, the voice of the **bridegroom**, and the voice of the bride, the voice of them that shall say, Praise the LORD of hosts: for the LORD is good; for his mercy endureth for ever: and of them that shall bring the sacrifice of praise into the house of the LORD. For I will cause to return the captivity of the land, as at the first, saith the LORD.

Thus saith the LORD of hosts; Again in this place, which is desolate without man and without beast, and in all the cities thereof, shall be an habitation of shepherds causing their flocks to lie down.

In the cities of the mountains, in the cities of the vale, and in the cities of the south, and in the land of Benjamin, and in the places about Jerusalem, and in the cities of Judah, shall the flocks pass again under the hands of him that telleth them, saith the LORD.

Behold, the days come, saith the LORD, that I will perform that good thing which I have promised unto the house of Israel and to the house of Judah.

These passages speak profoundly to our expectant hearts of peace, restoration, and divine fulfillment of promises both ancient and modern. The Guarantor of those blessings is the coming Bridegroom.

Alas, the divine guarantee of such remarkable blessings is not sufficient to overpower another divine gift—agency, or the power to act. Those who do not heed the call to prepare for the Bridegroom cannot receive the promised blessings. Such individuals have chosen to put themselves far away from the path of the wedding party, the coming kingdom of Heaven. Look at what the parable tells us: *all* ten virgins did go "forth to meet the bridegroom"—in other words, many, if not all of us, have every intention of meeting the Lord. Only those who have thoroughly prepared their vessels to take up their light and let it shine once the Bridegroom arrives will be allowed to join Him on the path that leads to the sacramental altar of the wedding feast.

Let's put this parable back into the context of Matthew 24–25 and see a few other key ideas. We remember that Christ had giving stern warnings and admonitions to His disciples about being prepared for the Day of the Lord. One of the themes that Christ stressed is that the disciples should "Watch therefore: for ye know not what hour your Lord doth come" (Matthew 24:42). Christ also strongly cautioned against the attitude, "My lord delayeth his coming" (Matthew 24:48), which leads to insobriety, oppression of one's neighbor, and ultimately to untrimmed lamps entirely lacking of sustaining oil.

This was the problem of the five foolish virgins. Though together with the five wise virgins they "went forth to meet the bridegroom" (Matthew 25:1), fully expecting to meet with the Lord while their lamps were yet burning, the Lord came in an hour that they did not expect. They felt that their meager supply for the initial journey to meet Him would be sufficient to take them to Him. Instead, from their perspective, He tarried. As a result, they were unprepared.

As is the reality of our spiritual journey, the Lord required that the virgins coming to meet Him were prepared with continual light, which comes through the purifying sacrifice of continual righteous living. They needed to be prepared not only for the first stages of the journey, but also the last. Thus through this parable, the Lord again urged His disciples to not be deceived but rather expectantly prepared to receive Him when He comes in great glory.

THE PARABLE OF THE TALENTS (MATTHEW 25:14–30)

Alerting His disciples to the perils of spiritual unpreparedness, Christ then issued another parable in the context of being ready for the Day of the Lord. A man (likely to be identified as the Lord) travels to a far country. Before doing so, he gathers his servants and gives each of them a talent. What is important to remember is that the talents were a divine gift, given to them by the Lord.

In the English language, we understand the word *talent* to refer those natural gifts and attributes that make up our character and abilities. However, the word *talent* in this sense refers to a sum of money; in fact, it is a rather large sum of money, perhaps equaling tens or hundreds of thousands of dollars in today's terms. After the servants received their allotted talents based on their ability (some five, some three, and some one), each was left to his own devices to do what he would with the talents entrusted to him.

Those servants entrusted with several talents exerted themselves to increase what they had. Through their efforts, these servants doubled their talents, and when their master returned, he rewarded them plentifully, even beyond comprehension. On the other hand, the one servant who had little did little with his talent. He hid away his talent and thus had nothing to offer his returning master. In consequence, the little that he did have was returned to the rightful owner—the Lord who was the giver of the gift. The Lord then delivered this talent to one who had displayed responsibility and effort with other God-given gifts.

If we take this story out of context, we may judge the Lord to be impartial, unfair, and even oppressive. But that is not at all what is going on with this carefully crafted parable suited for a particular context. Remember that the Lord is seeking to prepare His disciples (and us, by extension) for His glorious return. Through this and the other similar parables He is delivering to them the secrets of preparedness: Stay alert; watch and pray always; be not deceived; exert effort to do good with whatever gifts the Lord has given you; do not idle away your transitory time on earth, for the day of reckoning will take place; and if you have not improved your time while on earth, your just reward will be as the slothful servant who hid away his life in fear or in idleness. Several scriptures clearly express the main intent of this parable.

Alma 34:30–35

And now, my brethren, I would that, after ye have received so many witnesses, seeing that the holy scriptures testify of these things, ye come forth and bring fruit unto repentance.

Yea, I would that ye would come forth and harden not your hearts any longer; for behold, now is the time and the day of your salvation; and therefore, if ye will repent and harden not your hearts, immediately shall the great plan of redemption be brought about unto you.

For behold, this life is the time for men to prepare to meet God; yea, behold the day of this life is the day for men to perform their labors.

And now, as I said unto you before, as ye have had so many witnesses, therefore, I beseech of you that ye do not procrastinate the day of your repentance until the end; for after this day of life, which is given us to prepare for eternity, behold, if we do not improve our time while in this life, then cometh the night of darkness wherein there can be no labor performed.

Ye cannot say, when ye are brought to that awful crisis, that I will repent, that I will return to my God. Nay, ye cannot say this; for that same spirit which doth possess your bodies at the time that ye go out of this life, that same spirit will have power to possess your body in that eternal world.

For behold, if ye have procrastinated the day of your repentance even until death, behold, ye have become subjected to the spirit of the devil, and he doth seal you his; therefore, the Spirit of the Lord hath withdrawn from you, and hath no place in you, and the devil hath all power over you; and this is the final state of the wicked.

D&C 82:18–19

And all this for the benefit of the church of the living God, that every man may improve upon his talent, that every man may gain other talents, yea, even an hundred fold, to be cast into the Lord's storehouse, to become the common property of the whole church—

Every man seeking the interest of his neighbor, and doing all things with an eye single to the glory of God.

Each of us can reassess our lives, inventory the gifts and talents entrusted to us, and review the ways we have sought to increase our talents that they might glorify the Lord and light our lamps.

THE PARABLE OF THE SHEEP AND THE GOATS
(MATTHEW 25:31–46)

Christ comes to the close of His sermon regarding the coming kingdom of Heaven with one final parable. It is as though the three parables of this chapter are representative of stages of testing that we must go through to be admitted into the presence of the Lord. Of course, we must not forget that each of these three parables can also be rightly understood to refer to the same thing: being prepared through faith, righteousness, and good works to receive the Bridegroom and admittance into His coming kingdom.

First is the test of being prepared to receive the Bridegroom with lamps trimmed and ready when He comes. Next, if we are found worthy to partake of the wedding feast, we must then stand before Him and give an accounting of all our talents and how we improved our time while on the mortal journey. Finally, there will be a great sorting out of the sheep and the goats—images used by the Lord to offer some of the most seemingly simple, but ultimately profound remarks concerning the path of righteousness.

In this parable, the Lord states in no uncertain terms that there will be a great division at the last day when all people and nations stand before His throne. Some will be separated to His left; these are labeled goats. Others will be separated to His right; these are called His sheep. His sheep are those who have hearkened unto His voice throughout their lives and those who will hear the most glorious and desired words: "Come, ye blessed of my Father, inherit the kingdom prepared for you from the foundation of the world" (Matthew 25:34).

What differentiates the sheep from the goats? What are the criteria for such a resounding and final judgment for eternity? In the simplicity that marks the power of God's divine message of salvation, the Lord reveals the sure path to eternal life:

Matthew 25:35–36, 40

> For I was an hungred, and ye gave me meat: I was thirsty, and ye gave me drink: I was a stranger, and ye took me in:
>
> Naked, and ye clothed me: I was sick, and ye visited me: I was in prison, and ye came unto me. . . .
>
> And the King shall answer and say unto them, Verily I say unto you, Inasmuch as ye have done it unto one of the least of these my brethren, ye have done it unto me.

Let us trim our lamps brightly by placing our feet firmly on the path of unbridled charity as we increase our talents in the service of others and our God. May we then be found prepared, awake, and ready to receive our awaited Bridegroom.

ACTS 10–15: CONTINUING REVELATION

Early in this last dispensation, a resounding call went forth through the Prophet Joseph Smith that the message of the gospel should be preached to all people:

> Our missionaries are going forth to different nations, and in Germany, Palestine, New Holland, Australia, the East Indies, and other places, the Standard of Truth has been erected; no unhallowed hand can stop the work from progressing; persecutions may rage, mobs may combine, armies may assemble, calumny may defame, but the truth of God will go forth boldly, nobly, and independent, till it has penetrated every continent, visited every clime, swept every country, and sounded in every ear, till the purposes of God shall be accomplished, and the Great Jehovah shall say the work is done.[26]

The message of this quote is even more familiar than the quote itself. Indeed, missionary work is one of the most fundamental aspects of the restored gospel. Consider this: nearly all of the revelations in the Doctrine and Covenants that were received *before* the founding of The Church of Jesus Christ on April 6, 1830, reference in some way missionary work or the spreading forth of God's gospel kingdom. That special urgency to share the knowledge of the truth with all who have ears to hear and

---

[26] This was committed to writing by Joseph Smith in the Wentworth letter of 1842. Joseph Smith, *History of The Church of Jesus Christ of Latter-day Saints,* B. H. Roberts, ed., 2d ed. rev., 7 vols. (Salt Lake City: The Church of Jesus Christ of Latter-day Saints, 1932–1951), 4:540.

hearts to obey has only become stronger over the years. Hence, we have a missionary mindset and a missionary-oriented church. Thus it is nearly impossible to imagine keeping the precious gift of the gospel all to ourselves.

It is this type of mindset that we must understand if we are to fully appreciate the significant mindset transformation that occurred among the first Christians of the ancient Church as they shifted from a Jewish audience to a worldwide Gentile audience. This monumental shift of focus is documented in Acts 10–15.

In comparison to our present-day missionary mindset, early Christianity originally had a restricted understanding of what it meant to spread the gospel kingdom across the earth. Christ Himself revealed this fact to the Nephites when He visited them on the American continent. When He spoke of gathering all of His sheep into one fold, Christ identified the Nephites as the "other sheep." He then explained how the ancient Jews had misunderstood two things. First, they assumed that the "other sheep" referred to the Gentiles. Second, they failed to recognize that the Gentiles would be converted through their preaching.

> Verily I say unto you, that ye are they of whom I said: Other sheep I have which are not of this fold; them also I must bring, and they shall hear my voice; and there shall be one fold, and one shepherd. And they [the Jews] understood me not, for they supposed it had been the Gentiles; for they understood not that the Gentiles should be converted through their preaching. (3 Nephi 15:21–22)

Let's examine the ancient past to learn of "identity issues" among the Jews. This will help us understand some of the reasons why the first Christians, including the Twelve Apostles, did not immediately consider taking the gospel to the Gentiles. It will also give us a context for understanding some of the religious controversies that shaped Christianity in its first decades. Next, let's review the storyline and main ideas from Acts 10–15 to highlight the process of revelation—in other words, change—that occurred in the early Church with regards to the Gentiles and see how identity questions continued to be a pressing concern for the young Church of ancient times. Finally, let's read several scriptures illuminating the doctrine that "God is no respecter of persons" (Acts 10:34).

QUESTIONS OF IDENTITY AMONG THE JEWS

The Jewish people have perpetually dealt with questions of identity: What is a Jew? What does it mean to be a Jew? The answers have been legion. Yet unity on a single answer is still a fleeting desire.

How does the ever-relevant question of identity among the Jews have anything to do with preaching the gospel to the Gentiles? The short answer is that due to Jewish identity issues, the first Christians, including the Twelve Apostles, did not think to take the gospel to the Gentiles. It was only when revelation offered additional light and knowledge that old traditions were put aside and the Church blossomed among the Gentiles.

There are three main ways that Jewish identity has been established across the centuries: (1) genealogy, (2) belief and ritual, and (3) circumcision. These aspects of identity have been emphasized or deemphasized in a variety of ways, depending on need and circumstance over the years. And they have always produced new and unique manifestations of Judaism. Hence, no strand of Judaism at any time or in any context is ever *exactly* like any other strand of Judaism. Even a perpetual river is constantly different.

Let's look at a few examples of Jewish identity crises.

When the Jews returned to Jerusalem from Babylon around 520 BC, genealogy was one of the most important characteristics for establishing identity. This is manifest in the writings of both Ezra and Nehemiah. For example, Ezra 2 is a detailed genealogical account of the returning Jewish captives. At first glance, this kind of genealogical report may hold little interest. However, with some consideration we can discern Ezra's purpose in recording these crucial details.

When the Jews returned to Jerusalem, they had received specific religious and political privileges from their liberator, Cyrus the Persian emperor, and these privileges were contingent on Jewish identity. As the Jews began to enjoy these privileges, the neighboring Samaritans, who did not have such religious and political favors, began claiming that they were also true Jews. In order to secure their own privileges, it was necessary for the returning Jews to prove their identity by means of their Jewish genealogy, something that the Samaritans could not do. Belief alone would not have been sufficient for the Jews to establish identity, for anyone can profess belief.

At this same time, genealogy was also essential in determining which priestly families had right to the priesthood offices. We note in Ezra 2:61–62 that several Jewish priestly families who could not produce the proper genealogical records were denied access to priesthood offices, while those who could prove their priestly genealogy were granted their station and right to the priesthood.

This example highlights that when the identity crisis was between Jews and non-Jews who claimed to be Jews, the arguments focused on establishing Jewishness through genealogy. But when Jews argued with Jews over what it meant to be a Jew, belief and ritual became the main focus for establishing identity. These latter arguments have been the most heated, the most prolonged, and the most divisive, creating so many versions of Judaism and Jewish identity that even during the time of Jesus Christ, Judaism was fractured into competing sects just like Christianity is today.

To say that there was a "mainstream Judaism" in the first century AD is a bit misleading. Consider, for example, that during the time of Jesus were at least half a dozen (and likely more) forms of Judaism to which one could adhere: (1) Pharisaic, (2) Sadducean, (3) Christian, (4) Zealot, (5) Herodian, and (6) Essene/Qumran (the Dead Sea Scroll Community).

We usually fail to recognize this breathtaking diversity of belief and practice among the ancient Jews, partly because among the numerous sects of Judaism that did exist at the time of Christ, only a small number actually survived past the first century AD. In fact, the two main forms of Judaism that did survive over the centuries were Christianity and Pharisaic Judaism, the latter more commonly known today as Rabbinic Judaism. When we see early Christianity in its proper context as another ancient sect of Judaism, similar to how Mormonism is another "brand" of Christianity, we begin to understand some of the intense controversies that embroiled the early Church. We can see in scripture, especially in Acts 15, that the controversy over circumcision was very much an identity issue among various Jewish groups (Christian Jews vs. Pharisaic Jews) that argued over what constituted following God's true path.

The centuries prior to Christianity help us understand how the debate over circumcision became such a key identity issue among the Jews. When the Greek armies conquered the Mediterranean and Mesopotamian world around 320 BC, Greek culture soon became a dominant, if not highly appealing, way to live life. The Jews residing in Jerusalem and throughout Palestine had mixed reactions to this new culture. Significantly, the present-day cultural tensions between East and West, particularly among Muslim nations encountering Western culture, are surprisingly similar to what we find in the histories of Jewish interaction with Greek and Roman culture.

In the face of Hellenization, some ancient Jews tried to keep to ancestral ways. Others, for various reasons (such as political and material opportunities), saw the advantages of adopting Greek culture. One of the standard institutions of Greek culture was the gymnasium, and it became for the Jews a center of debate over identity. Why? Greeks valued the power and beauty of the body. The gymnasium was the place where one would exercise and display the full beauty of body—naked. By the way, the Greek word *gymnos*, from which the word *gymnasium* derives, means "naked." Remember that the Greeks did not practice circumcision; the Jews did. The difference became obvious at the gymnasium.

Those Jews who wanted to look like the Greeks at the gymnasium stopped practicing circumcision. Other Jews, who did not care for the intrusions of foreign Greek culture, strongly believed that rejecting circumcision was a total betrayal of the covenants God had made with the Jews, covenants that had been signed in the flesh since the days of Abraham. Eventually, this debate solidified the idea among many Jews that only those who have been marked in the flesh through circumcision were the true inheritors of the blessings and promises of God.

With this in mind, we can begin to understand why some of the Jewish Christians were so upset at the thought of including Gentiles in the covenants and promises of the Lord without also requiring that these Gentiles wear the sign of the covenant—circumcision (see especially Acts 15). Yet, what we will see is that baptism and receiving the Holy Ghost became the new mark of the covenant between God and His people.

One final example of how belief and ritual defined Jewishness, and which informs our understanding of Acts 10–15, is the debate over cleanliness according to the law of Moses. The Pharisaic Jews, progenitors of Rabbinic Judaism, strongly believed that their interpretation of cleanliness was most acceptable to God. They exerted much effort to persuade all Jews to live according to their interpretation. In dealing with the idea of separating clean from the unclean, they taught that this meant that Jews and non-Jews should not eat together.

Originally, this was probably a practical consideration, since foreigners may eat foods that are unclean and, if the table is shared, doing so would pollute the ritually clean food of the Jews, thus rendering the Jews incapable of performing the required sacred duties of worship prescribed in the holy scriptures.

Over the years as the Jews learned to live under Greek and then Roman rule, many tried to maintain the ritual cleanliness of their food by not eating with the Gentiles (in other words, foreigners). As time went on, many of the Jews did not think it abnormal that they did not share table fellowship with foreigners. In William Shakespeare's *The Merchant of Venice*, the Jewish antagonist Shylock refuses to eat with his Christian business partners with this exclamation: "[T]o smell pork, to eat of the habitation of which your prophet the Nazarite [i.e., Christ], conjured the devil into! I will buy with you, sell with you, talk with you, walk with you, and so following; but I will not eat with you, drink with you, nor pray with you."

Fifteen hundred years after the time of Jesus's apostles, then, the same issue was still seen as a dividing line between religious adherents— possibly as much in the view of Christians, such as Shakespeare, as in the eyes of the Jews, supposedly represented by Shylock.[27]

This same religious feeling also informed the Jewish attitude of not sharing the gospel with Gentiles. If we understand the gospel brotherhood as a family sitting down to share a pure meal together, we can begin to understand why the Jews did not readily think to invite "unclean" guests to the banquet. We will see in Acts that early members of the Church had this idea about the Gentiles, even to the point that they did not consider the possibility of sharing the gospel with the Gentiles until additional light and knowledge was received through revelation.

In light of this religious and cultural background surrounding the Jewish identity questions, let's learn of the work of God to all His children as expressed in Acts 10–15.

---

[27] This idea was suggested to me by my wife, Lisa Maren Rampton Halverson.

REVELATION IN THE ANCIENT CHURCH—ACTS 10

Acts 10 describes for us the manner and circumstances in which Peter's heart was changed concerning taking the gospel to the Gentiles. One day while residing in Joppa, a port city on the Mediterranean Sea (just south of modern day Tel-Aviv), Peter went to his rooftop to pray. As he prayed, he became hungry. Then a symbolic vision opened to him. He saw a vessel full of all types of animals descend from heaven accompanied by a command, "Rise, Peter; kill, and eat." The animals in this version are not fully described in terms of clean and unclean. Nevertheless it is certain that to Peter they represented animals recognized as "unclean" in Jewish tradition.

Peter resisted. Why? As a Jew of his time, he had been raised to believe that ritual purity was of great importance, so eating ritually unclean animals was unacceptable. Influenced by his religious upbringing, Peter resisted transgressing the boundaries he had known throughout his life. Yet the vision from heaven persisted, and three times the animals were offered as food to Peter. Each time that he resisted, a voice from heaven persuaded Peter to see God's work in a new light: "What God hath cleansed, that call not thou common" (Acts 10:15).

Soon after the vision passed, Peter heard a knock at the door. Messengers from a Gentile named Cornelius waited outside. Several days before, Cornelius had received an angelic visit encouraging him to hear Peter preach. So Cornelius sent his servants to invite Peter to preach to him. Realizing that the animals of his vision were symbols of the Gentiles pronounced clean by God, Peter heartily agreed to visit Cornelius.

Peter traveled from Joppa to the thoroughly gentile city of Caesarea Maritima (about 40 miles north of Joppa up the Mediterranean coast) to share the gospel message with Cornelius, his household, and his friends. It was at the home of Cornelius that Peter spoke the truth that only the day before he had learned for himself: "Of a truth I perceive that God is no respecter of persons" (Acts 10:34). Peter had learned that what he had previously understood to be common and unclean (being a Gentile) was in reality, and by the voice of God, clean.

Even though Peter had been taught throughout his life to refrain from sitting at the same table with that which was unclean (Gentiles), suddenly new light caused him to recognize that all of God's children were deserving of hearing the Good News. So the gospel message began to spread out among the Gentiles from that time forward. Jewish converts to Christianity marveled at the outpouring of the Holy Ghost that fell upon the new Gentile converts, exclaiming, "Can any man forbid water, that these should not be baptized, which have received the Holy Ghost as well as we?" (Acts 10:47).

REVELATION, CHANGE, AND GROWTH—ACTS 11

Even though Peter received a powerful revelation to extend the blessings of the gospel to all worthy Gentiles, many Jewish Christians in Jerusalem needed to hear the new revelation, receive a witness of its truth, and open their hearts to changing their minds, changing their behaviors, and changing their attitudes. It is interesting to note, in this light, that the Greek word used throughout the New Testament for *repentance* (*metanoia*) literally means "to have a change of mind." Change, however, is not often an easy undertaking, and it's one that is usually met with resistance.

When Peter arrived in Jerusalem to report on his preaching to the Gentiles, resistance greeted him. Luke labels these resisters as "they of the circumcision" (in other words, Jewish converts to Christianity who likely wished to maintain circumcision as a feature of identity). This group showed the same types of resistance to interacting with the Gentiles as did Peter—the Jewish fear of mingling clean with unclean. They accused Peter, saying, "Thou wentest in to men uncircumcised, and didst eat with them" (Acts 11:3).

Peter well understood their concern and resistance; he had experienced it himself until recently. Instead of rebuking their antagonism or criticizing their mindset before they had the benefit of new light and knowledge, he shared his personal testimony of revelation and change.

When Peter was finished with his witness of new revelation, "they held their peace, and glorified God, saying, Then hath God also to the Gentiles granted repentance unto life" (Acts 11:18). They too were touched by this revelation, which brought about a change of mind and a change of heart. When the Jewish Christians at Jerusalem recognized that this was a revelation from God, they ultimately received it with rejoicing.

The rest of Acts 11 covers at least a year of missionary activity among the Gentiles after the revelation was received. During that time, the work spread among many of the Greeks living in the Roman Empire, especially in the large and busy commercial city of Antioch (on the north eastern corner of the Mediterranean sea about 300 miles north of Jerusalem). It was in Antioch that Paul began and ended many of his missionary travels, and it was from the converts in Antioch that Jewish Christians received food and aid during a famine in Jerusalem (see Acts 11:29).

There is an important detail in this chapter that is often overlooked. According to Luke's record, "the disciples were called Christians first in Antioch" (Acts 11:26). Notice that this name is first applied to Gentile converts, not Jewish converts. In other words, the Jewish disciples of Jesus Christ (whom we today call "Early Christians," along with all others who followed Christ) did not see themselves as part of a religion or movement separate or distinct from Judaism. In fact, they believed that they were the true expression of Judaism.

Only later, and in contention with Pharisaic Judaism, which itself evolved into Rabbinic Judaism, did disciples of Jesus Christ consider themselves separate from Judaism and representative of an entirely new (revealed and restored) religion, which they called "Christianity." The closest analogy we have to express this phenomenon is to look at the Christian movement today known as Mormonism. We of course understand ourselves to be but one Christian group among many; we certainly do not identify ourselves outside of the realm of Christianity. Yet, like the Jewish disciples of Jesus Christ who saw themselves as following the truth path of Judaism, Mormons see themselves as following the true path of Christianity. It was only decades after the initial movements of Christianity that the early Christians began to define themselves as a separate and distinct religion with a name to separate themselves from other groups.

GROWTH AND PERSECUTION—ACTS 12

With any new movement, particularly one that is growing and successful, resistance will mount and persecution will follow. We saw it in the early days of the Restored Church, and it certainly occurred among the first Christians. Just as Joseph Smith was falsely incarcerated from time to time, so too was Peter, the leader of the early saints, falsely accused, jailed, and then miraculously released by an angel. Just as it was anciently, so it is today. There will always be those who oppose the works of righteousness. Yet the Lord has declared, "Remember, remember that it is not the work of God that is frustrated, but the work of men" (D&C 3:3). God will continue to frustrate the work of men as they attempt frustrate the work of God. They are only kicking against the pricks.

We should also note that the patterns of restoration that occurred in ancient days among the Christians and that are found in Acts 10–12 have been repeated in this last dispensation. Any time a restoration occurs, so too do visions, persecutions, conversions, pentecostal outpourings of the Spirit, manifestations of the gifts of the Spirit, preaching of the gospel, revelation, and mighty acts of charity and consecration.

MISSIONARY WORK THROUGHOUT THE WORLD—ACTS 13 AND 14

Even though the Church had received the revelation that all worthy Gentiles could be taught the gospel, missionary labors were most fruitful when they began in areas with established Jewish communities. This is what we find in the book of Acts.

Beginning around 600 BC and continuing even until our present day, and mostly due to political pressures or economic or lifestyle advantages, Jews have established communities in diverse locations. All of this moving around, emigrating, immigrating, and establishing of new communities in diverse locations also plays a major role in the many identity crises experienced by the Jews. With the rise of the Greek-ruled states around 300 BC and then the rise of the Roman Empire throughout the Middle East around 70 BC, this process was magnified as Jews were incorporated into an ever-expanding and pluralistic society. Jewish communities and settlements blossomed and thrived all over the ancient world from North Africa to Egypt and the Arabian Peninsula, the fertile lands of the Mesopotamian plain, throughout Asia Minor (modern-day Turkey), and throughout the lands and islands of Greece, Italy, Gaul (modern-day France), and Spain.

The brotherhood of Judaism was a worldwide phenomenon that facilitated fraternity and missionary work in many areas. When Christian missionaries set forth to share the message of the gospel in new cities and lands, they often started their efforts among the Jewish communities, preaching first in their synagogues. This is akin to what many of the early Mormon missionaries did when they spread the message abroad: they went first to their family, friends, and religious associates, often meeting in churches and religious halls to share the message of the Restored gospel. The ancient Christian missionaries did the same thing.

They first shared their message among their Jewish friends at the various synagogues through the Mediterranean world. Once the message got established in these communities, inroads were also made among the Gentile inhabitants of those same areas.

What we have in Acts 13 is an instance of this type of missionary work. Paul and Barnabas first began to preach the gospel message in synagogues in various locations. But resistance followed. Like the missionaries in the Book of Mormon who had to contend with false prophets and wily lawyers, Paul and Barnabas called down the powers of heaven to strike a false prophet with blindness that he might no longer impede the work of the Lord. It is a fruitful study to compare this story in Acts 13:4–13 with similar missionary stories found in the Book of Mormon, such as those in Jacob 7, Alma 11, and Alma 30.

Acts 13 is also a rich that helps us understand the preaching techniques used by early Christian missionaries, such as Paul, to encourage people to follow the path of Christ. For example, in Acts 13 Paul preaches the gospel message to fellow Jews in a synagogue in Asia Minor. He crafts his message by recounting the sacred history of Israel from the time of Egyptian bondage down to his present day, explaining how Christ is the fulfillment of the promises and prophecies found throughout the Old Testament.

A similar technique is found throughout the Book of Mormon. One powerful example is that of Nephi's exhortations to his brothers (see 1 Nephi 17:23–55). The mighty promise of the Book of Mormon found in Moroni 10:3–5 is based on this technique as well—though in this particular case, Moroni does not have the space to review the sacred history. Instead, he encourages the reader to remember sacred history, which results in the reader dwelling on the great goodness of God. Most significantly, the reader is then prepared to feel the Spirit testify of the truth.

As many Gentiles flocked to the truth as preached by Paul, some of the Jews became jealous over Paul's growing popularity. These Jews resisted him and persuaded the influential and wealthy individuals of the city to expel the Christian missionaries. But Paul was not dissuaded, and the work continued in other cities among the Gentiles who received the message with gladness. The Jewish rejection and the Gentile acceptance of the gospel may be compared to what occurred in the Nephite civilization when the Lamanites finally had the gospel preached to them. They received it with open hearts while the Nephites rejected the call to repentance.

Acts 14 contains a sobering account of persecution against Paul and his associates to the point that Jews in Antioch and Iconium stoned Paul. Though left for dead, he was revived, and he continued his missionary efforts as before. In this regard, Paul was like Timothy, the brother of Nephi, who not many years before Christ's visit to the Americas was stoned to death only to later be miraculously revived by Nephi (see 3 Nephi 7:19; 19:4).

ACTS 15

Earlier we discussed some of the reasons why circumcision was such a decisive factor for Jewish identity. Acts 15 portrays this sharp debate in full relief and spells out why it led to quite a controversy in the early Christian church. Apparently some of the Jewish converts to Christianity had gone among the Gentiles preaching that if they were to be saved, they needed circumcision, the ancient mark of the covenant.

Paul, Barnabas, and other Church leaders recognized this erroneous idea. They knew that Christ had set mankind free from the outward performances of the law through faith on the name of Jesus Christ and that faith was to be manifest through repentance, baptism, reception of the Holy Ghost, and enduring to the end. At a general conference of the Church at Jerusalem, the brethren discussed the matter and came to a common consensus. In unity, the brethren sent an epistle to the gentile churches clarifying that circumcision and the law of Moses were not binding requirements on converts to Christianity.

It is interesting to note that the law of Moses with its minutia and exceedingly detailed laws was replaced for all followers of Christ, Jew and Gentile alike, with prescriptions as simple and short as the Noahide laws (see Genesis 9:1–7).[28] The brethren wrote in their reasoned epistle thus (see especially verse 29 for the list of "laws" Christians should live):

> The apostles and elders and brethren send greeting unto the brethren which are of the Gentiles in Antioch and Syria and Cilicia:
> Forasmuch as we have heard, that certain which went out from us have troubled you with words, subverting your souls,

---

[28] Indeed, the simple rules and regulations listed in Acts 15:29 do resemble the Noahide law to refrain from eating blood.

saying, Ye must be circumcised, and keep the law: to whom we gave no such commandment:

It seemed good unto us, being assembled with one accord, to send chosen men unto you with our beloved Barnabas and Paul,

Men that have hazarded their lives for the name of our Lord Jesus Christ.

We have sent therefore Judas and Silas, who shall also tell you the same things by mouth.

For it seemed good to the Holy Ghost, and to us, to lay upon you no greater burden than these necessary things;

That ye abstain from meats offered to idols, and from blood, and from things strangled, and from fornication: from which if ye keep yourselves, ye shall do well. Fare ye well. (Acts 15:23–29)

GOD IS NO RESPECTER OF PERSONS

It is rewarding to learn of the very real and human challenges that the early Church faced, for through these experiences they left recorded for us a most powerful doctrinal truth that God is no respecter of persons. This doctrine, however, is not original to the early Christian church, nor has the Lord failed to repeat this message in succeeding generations. Several scriptural passages enlarge our understanding of this wholesome doctrine.

1 Nephi 17:35

Behold, the Lord esteemeth all flesh in one; he that is righteous is favored of God.

Alma 26:37

Now my brethren, we see that God is mindful of every people, whatsoever land they may be in; yea, he numbereth his people, and his bowels of mercy are over all the earth. Now this is my joy, and my great thanksgiving; yea, and I will give thanks unto my God forever. Amen.

Acts 15:7–11

Peter rose up, and said unto them, Men and brethren, ye know how that a good while ago God made choice among us, that the Gentiles by my mouth should hear the word of the gospel, and believe.

And God, which knoweth the hearts, bare them witness, giving them the Holy Ghost, even as he did unto us;

And put no difference between us and them, purifying their hearts by faith.

Now therefore why tempt ye God, to put a yoke upon the neck of the disciples, which neither our fathers nor we were able to bear?

But we believe that through the grace of the Lord Jesus Christ we shall be saved, even as they.

Acts 17:26

[God] hath made of one blood all nations of men for to dwell on all the face of the earth, and hath determined the times before appointed, and the bounds of their habitation.

Romans 2:10–11

Glory, honour, and peace, to every man that worketh good, to the Jew first, and also to the Gentile:

For there is no respect of persons with God.

Romans 10:11–13

For the scripture saith, Whosoever believeth on him shall not be ashamed.

For there is no difference between the Jew and the Greek: for the same Lord over all is rich unto all that call upon him.

For whosoever shall call upon the name of the Lord shall be saved.

D&C 1:31–35

I the Lord cannot look upon sin with the least degree of allowance;

Nevertheless, he that repents and does the commandments of the Lord shall be forgiven;

And he that repents not, from him shall be taken even the light which he has received; for my Spirit shall not always strive with man, saith the Lord of Hosts.

And again, verily I say unto you, O inhabitants of the earth: I the Lord am willing to make these things known unto all flesh;

For I am no respecter of persons. . . .

May we follow in the steps of the Lord, esteeming all flesh in one as we carry the message and blessings of the gospel throughout the world.

ACTS 21–28: FAITHFULLY WITNESS OF CHRIST

THE FINAL CHAPTERS OF ACTS present us with an enormous amount of information—historical, geographical and doctrinal—as it follows the last years of Paul's earthly ministry. The following brief outline of these eight chapters will first offer a few insights into the religious and social tensions simmering in the days of Paul and how his work to preach the gospel to Jew and gentile alike landed him in hot water because of these tensions. Second, it will draw parallels between Paul and Christ, their ministry, testimony, and suffering at the hands of authorities. In these chapters pay attention to the diverse audiences and opportunities Paul had to preach the message of Christ, and consider how Paul's missionary efforts were the fulfillment of many promises and revelations.

ACTS 21

We begin in the city of Miletus, though Acts 21:1 does not make that clear; we learn in Acts 20:15 that Paul had arrived in Miletus. Where is Miletus? During the days of Paul it was a city of western Asia Minor (modern-day Turkey), near the coast. It is there we pick up the story of Paul visiting various cities, bidding farewell to Saints, and encouraging them with the truths of the gospel as he heads to Jerusalem.

Once Paul reached the coast of Palestine at the Roman port city of Caesarea Maritima (a city built by Herod the Great and dedicated to Emperor Caesar Augustus as a form of flattery), a prophet by the name of Agabus offered ill tidings that Paul would be bound in chains if he proceeded to Jerusalem. Undeterred by such a prophecy of woe, Paul left for Jerusalem, "ready not to be bound only, but also to die at Jerusalem for the name of the Lord Jesus" (Acts 21:13).

At Jerusalem the Saints received him with much rejoicing, but not without concern, for there was still religious controversy swirling in the air among the various Jewish groups. Hence Paul's missionary activities were under scrutiny. The inter-Jewish strife was, at its core, an identity issue. For centuries, the Jews had identified themselves as a covenant people. The outward, physical sign for such fellowship among men was circumcision. Paul, though a Jew and likely circumcised, taught that Christian Jews and Gentiles need not be bound to the ancient custom of circumcision. Instead, they were free in Christ. The sign of this covenantal freedom would be the gifts of the Spirit, particularly the gift of charity (see 1 Corinthians 12–13) manifested after baptism and the reception of the Holy Ghost.

Many Jews, even those who professed to be Christians, were incensed over such a doctrine, which they felt worked against the very identity standards that had been venerated for centuries. Understanding this turmoil and conflict, the brethren of the Church in Jerusalem requested that Paul try to reduce the concerns of those Jewish Christians not yet able to find room in their hearts and minds for the additional light and knowledge of revelation. Being willing to accommodate others, he accompanied several Jewish Christians at their purification rituals for their Nazarite vows, which had long been a sign of Jewish devotion to God throughout the centuries. (As you'll remember, Samson was strong as long as he kept his Nazarite vows; he became weak when he broke his vows.) Many hoped that by showing this outward sign of Jewishness, Paul would appease the controversy and questioning over his alleged destruction of Jewish identity through the preaching of the gospel.

Unfortunately, Paul's motives to overcome the misunderstandings and prejudices of others were, not surprisingly, misunderstood. Whatever contention and outrage had been simmering below the surface in Jerusalem suddenly exploded to the extent that it sent shock waves throughout the Roman Empire. While Paul was in the temple accompanying four men going through the Nazarite purification ritual, other Jews accused Paul of bringing Greek Gentiles into the temple. From our perspective, of course, we know that Paul had done no such thing. But some, whether through ignorance, misunderstanding, or maliciousness, accused Paul of defiling the temple. What happened next is sometimes a little difficult for us to comprehend in our Western democracies, where we generally seek to let the rule of reason and order dictate our response to social outrage.

Why was having a Gentile enter sacred space at the Jewish temple viewed by the Jews as such an atrocity? During the days of Paul, the Jewish collective consciousness was still seared with the memory of their oppression and defilement under Greek rule, which had occurred only two hundred years earlier (around 167 BC). Under the oppressive rule of Antiochus IV, the Jews were required to sacrifice pigs and establish abominations of desolation in the temple (for example, erect altars to the worship of Greek gods). That's not all. According to 2 Maccabees 3 in the Apocrypha, a Greek general defiled the temple in Jerusalem by attempting to enter the Holy of Holies and steal the sacred temple funds. These things were the greatest affront to Jewish piety, identity, purity, dignity, and respect. Ever after, anyone who crossed—or even *appeared* to cross—these boundaries was threatened with the most brutal punishments.

With this in the back of their collective consciousness, many of the Jews at the temple rushed Paul, dragged him out of the temple, and began to beat him mercilessly, intending to kill him. They would have succeeded had not the Roman tribune (chief captain) who was in charge of keeping order at the Jewish temple rushed the crowd with his centurions and soldiers to break up the confusion. Paul, the one who had "caused" the pandemonium, was immediately seized and shackled. The tribune sought to discover the cause of the matter, but the crowd was shouting in such intolerable and indecipherable competition that the soldiers then carried Paul into the nearby fortress, both to protect him from the mob and to ascertain just what had lit the flame to begin with.

One professor of ancient Greek commented to me, in trying to explain the riot Paul found himself in, that such interminable confusion of shouting voices and the violent reactions of mobocracy are still seen— much to the horror of Western observers—among the people of the Middle East today. Everyone speaks at once, each attempting to be heard over the others. Considering such behavior, it is no wonder that some Jewish groups, such as those at Qumran (of the Dead Sea Scrolls fame), withdrew and formed their own societies where rules of civility dictated that only one person speak at a time. This rule was so highly regarded at Qumran that disobedience could result in the individual being thrust from the community.

The tribune was surprised when he heard Paul speaking Greek; he was more surprised to discover that Paul was a citizen of Tarsus, a prominent city. With this knowledge, the tribune granted Paul's request to address the thronging mob below. Some historical and cultural context helps us understand what happened next.

When the tribune realized that Paul spoke Greek, he remarked that Paul must certainly not be the Egyptian Jew who raised a revolt against the Romans beforehand. Church historian Eusebius of Caesarea (fourth century AD) provides more information about that rebel Egyptian Jew:

> But the Jews were afflicted with a greater plague than these by the Egyptian false prophet. For there appeared in the land an impostor who aroused faith in himself as a prophet, and collected about thirty thousand of those whom he had deceived, and led them from the desert to the so-called Mount of Olives whence he was prepared to enter Jerusalem by force and to overpower the Roman garrison and seize the government of the people, using those who made the attack with him as body guards. But Felix anticipated his attack, and went out to meet him with the Roman legionaries, and all the people joined in the defense, so that when the battle was fought the Egyptian fled with a few followers, but the most of them were destroyed or taken captive.[29]

Considering these events, which took place in the time of Felix, we can see how volatile the region was and how susceptible it was to religious riots.

ACTS 22

Even though he spoke Greek, Paul addressed this outrageous mob in Hebrew, which brought them to silence. In his defense, he explained how his own zealousness for the law of Moses had been converted to zealousness for the things of Christ. The underlying Greek word for defense is *apologia*, hence the word "apologetics." Our word *apology* derives from the Greek *apologia* but does not retain the strong sense of

---

[29] *Eusebius Church History*, Book 3 chapter 21, section 1, in *A Select Library of Nicene and Post-Nicene Fathers of the Christian Church, Second Series*, Translated by Philip Schaff and Henry Wace (New York: Charles Scribner's Sons), 123.

verbally defending oneself against accusations. Those with ears to hear could likely understand that their angry physical rage against Paul was akin to Paul's former career as a Pharisee who persecuted Christian Jews, delivering them over to the Jewish authorities for punishment.

Paul spoke of the Lord appearing to him in the temple, commanding him to spread the gospel among the Gentiles. At that point his defense was cut short: as soon as they heard the combination of the words *Lord*, *temple*, and *Gentiles*, the angry Jewish mob raged against Paul again, clamoring for his death.

Paul had obviously not abated the angry Jewish crowds, which the Roman guards were deeply anxious to quell. One of the centurions decided to solve the problem by flogging Paul to receive the truth concerning the ongoing uproar. Paul, with his wit and wisdom still intact and knowing how to masterfully address each specific audience, claimed exemption from flogging because he was a Roman citizen. With this, Paul was unshackled and spared the rod.

ACTS 23–24

The next day Paul was arraigned before the Roman representatives and the Jewish Sanhedrin—the Jewish political leadership, including the high priests, the chief priests, and the most important political and religious leaders from the Sadducees and Pharisees. Paul's "defense" to these Jewish nobles was noticeably different from his address to the Jewish mobs. Instead of describing his spiritual conversion, he stated with simplicity that he had a clear conscience before God. Joseph Smith made a similar statement on his way to his martyrdom: "I am going like a lamb to the slaughter; but I am calm as a summer's morning; I have a conscience void of offense towards God, and towards all men" (D&C 135:4).

Illegally, the chief high priest had Paul slapped for such a statement. Paul responded, like Christ did before him, in describing the corrupt spiritual leaders of Israel "thou whited wall," referring to whitewashed sepulchers full of dead men's bones visible just outside the city walls of Jerusalem (Matthew 23:27). But then seizing the moment, Paul sized up his audience with the recognition that he was addressing a religiously divided council; some were Pharisees, some were Sadducees. So he claimed to believe in the resurrection of the dead.

The doctrine of resurrection is core to the Jewish Christian message, but it was also a central tenet of the Jewish Pharisees. On the other hand, Jewish Sadducees did not believe in a resurrection. Suddenly there was a great tumult among the Jewish leaders. Just moments earlier the two groups had been united in their anger toward Paul. Now they were divided against each other along theological lines, and they quickly forgot why they had convened in the first place. Again, the Roman authorities had to deliver Paul from the harm of his angry brethren.

Though Paul was put into custody again, he was not alone. That night the Lord appeared to him. After encouraging Paul to be of good cheer, the Lord delivered a most important revelation: "As thou has testified of me in Jerusalem, so must thou bear witness also at Rome" (Acts 23:11). We can only wonder how such a revelation may have affected Paul. Still, this revelation would not be fulfilled for nearly three years , which must have seemed a lengthy period of time to Paul.

As a Roman citizen, Paul had certain privileges. Among those was the right to protection of Roman authorities and the opportunity for a court hearing. When the tribune discovered that a plot was forming to murder Paul, he quickly sent Paul under the protection of hundreds of soldiers from Jerusalem to Caesarea where Felix, the Roman procurator or governor of Judea, was stationed. Felix agreed to hear the case and summoned the Jewish rulers from Jerusalem to testify against Paul.

The Jewish rulers came from Jerusalem with deceitful intent. They accused Paul of being a Nazarene (in other words, a Christian), raising a tumult in the temple, and causing sedition throughout Jerusalem and Judea. In his own defense, Paul confessed that he was a follower of Christ but that he likewise believed and followed the law and the prophets. He then explained that his belief in the resurrection of the dead was no different or strange than what other Jewish groups (such as the Pharisees) freely believed. And, Paul concluded, it was for expressing this belief before the Jewish elders that they sought to kill him.

Felix well understood the theological differences among the Jews, likely because his own wife was a Jew. Felix recognized that these differences were not sufficient to bring about a punishment of death. Instead, Felix summoned Lysias, the Roman tribune at Jerusalem, to give his perspective on the disturbance that occurred.

Acts does not indicate whether Lysias came to Caesarea. What we do learn is that Paul shared the gospel message with Felix and his wife, but then *was left in prison for two years*. Felix apparently had two reasons for leaving Paul in prison for so long. First, Felix hoped that Paul had rich friends who would "pay bail"—in other words, "bribe" Felix to let Paul go; Felix was hoping to make money off Paul. Second, and this is related to the first reason, Felix sought to gain the favor of the people of Judea who Paul had incensed.

ACTS 25

After two years, the Romans appointed a new governor over Judea, and Porcius Festus replaced Felix. Festus also attempted to discover the truth of the matter against Paul. Was Paul truly worthy of death, as many of the Jews proclaimed? Or was it simply an internal disorder due to theological differences?

In an attempt to discover the truth, Festus gathered the Jewish leaders who had originally accused Paul of sedition and treachery. The same charges as before were again leveled against Paul. But Festus was not able to determine the reliability and accuracy of such statements, so he wanted to take Paul from the Roman provincial capital of Judea, located at Caesarea Maritima, back to Jerusalem for further questioning. Again Paul used Roman law and citizenship to appeal his case, this time to Caesar. Nero may have been the Roman Emperor at this time. Paul knew that he had done no wrong to the Jewish people, and he feared a bigoted trial at Jerusalem.

So it was determined that Paul would go to Rome and to Caesar. But before leaving, Paul had more opportunities to share the gospel of Christ with many people, including rulers. For example, King Agrippa and his wife, Bernice, came to visit Festus, who told them Paul's story. The Jews had a *de facto* or nominal king and queen at this time, but the Romans were the ultimate authority. (This is somewhat akin to Great Britain having a parliament of elected officials while retaining a figurehead of king and queen.) Agrippa and Bernice wished to hear Paul speak, so Festus gathered an audience to fulfill their wish. He also wanted to see if anyone could help him find a good reason to send Paul to Caesar, since it was a terrible political liability for a Roman governor to send a prisoner to Caesar without reason or cause.

It is important to note that Festus as procurator held the same position as Pontius Pilate. Pontius Pilate had exclaimed to the Jews of Christ, "Ye have brought this man unto me, as one that perverteth the people: and, behold, I, having examined him before you, have found no fault in this man touching those things whereof ye accuse him" (Luke 23:14). In a similar sentiment, Festus testified that Paul was innocent of perverting the people: "I found that he had committed nothing worthy of death" (Acts 25:25).

ACTS 26

As he had done on so many other occasions, several which are recorded in Acts 21–28, Paul shared his conversion story. His witness was simple yet thorough: like his current antagonists, he too had once persecuted Christians from city to city, even unto physical death. But the Lord had appeared to him in a light "above the brightness of the sun" and commanded him to share the gospel of Christ with Jew and Gentile alike, just as the law and the prophets had made known. Like Paul, Joseph Smith had also seen a powerful vision above the brightness of the sun and would not deny it; in the same way, Paul refused to say or teach anything but the truth.

Compare Paul's experience to what we read in Joseph Smith—History 1:21–25:

> Some few days after I had this vision, I happened to be in company with one of the Methodist preachers, who was very active in the before mentioned religious excitement; and, conversing with him on the subject of religion, I took occasion to give him an account of the vision which I had had. I was greatly surprised at his behavior; he treated my communication not only lightly, but with great contempt, saying it was all of the devil, that there were no such things as visions or revelations in these days; that all such things had ceased with the apostles, and that there would never be any more of them.
>
> I soon found, however, that my telling the story had excited a great deal of prejudice against me among professors of religion, and was the cause of great persecution, which continued to increase; and though I was an obscure boy, only between fourteen and fifteen years of age, and my circumstances in life such as to

make a boy of no consequence in the world, yet men of high standing would take notice sufficient to excite the public mind against me, and create a bitter persecution; and this was common among all the sects—all united to persecute me.

It caused me serious reflection then, and often has since, how very strange it was that an obscure boy, of a little over fourteen years of age, and one, too, who was doomed to the necessity of obtaining a scanty maintenance by his daily labor, should be thought a character of sufficient importance to attract the attention of the great ones of the most popular sects of the day, and in a manner to create in them a spirit of the most bitter persecution and reviling. But strange or not, so it was, and it was often the cause of great sorrow to myself.

However, it was nevertheless a fact that I had beheld a vision. I have thought since, that I felt much like Paul, when he made his defense before King Agrippa, and related the account of the vision he had when he saw a light, and heard a voice; but still there were but few who believed him; some said he was dishonest, others said he was mad; and he was ridiculed and reviled. But all this did not destroy the reality of his vision. He had seen a vision, he knew he had, and all the persecution under heaven could not make it otherwise; and though they should persecute him unto death, yet he knew, and would know to his latest breath, that he had both seen a light and heard a voice speaking unto him, and all the world could not make him think or believe otherwise.

So it was with me. I had actually seen a light, and in the midst of that light I saw two Personages, and they did in reality speak to me; and though I was hated and persecuted for saying that I had seen a vision, yet it was true; and while they were persecuting me, reviling me, and speaking all manner of evil against me falsely for so saying, I was led to say in my heart: Why persecute me for telling the truth? I have actually seen a vision; and who am I that I can withstand God, or why does the world think to make me deny what I have actually seen? For I had seen a vision; I knew it, and I knew that God knew it, and I could not deny it, neither dared I do it; at least I knew that by so doing I would offend God, and come under condemnation.

While hearing Paul's lucid testimony, Festus exclaimed that Paul was crazy. Jesus was also accused of being a lunatic (see John 10:19–21), and like his Master before him, Paul was falsely accused yet again. Yet, so powerful was Paul's testimony that even King Agrippa was nearly persuaded to be a Christian. Afterwards, Agrippa shared with Festus his private conclusion, concurring with Festus that "This man doeth nothing worthy of death or of bonds" (Acts 26:31). Agrippa then lamented, "This man might have been set at liberty, if he had not appealed unto Caesar" (Acts 26:32).

ACTS 27

Revelation was to be fulfilled: Paul was to preach the gospel in Rome. Together with hundreds of others (some of whom were also prisoners), Paul set sail for Italy. Along the way he had opportunities to teach and preach of Christ and to prophesy. At one point en route to Italy, the ship was threatened by nature. Paul urged everyone to stay with the ship, and he prophesied that not one individual would be lost if they heeded his counsel.

The passengers obeyed Paul; the ship ran aground and broke apart on the island Melita (known today as the island of Malta). The bay where Paul shipwrecked is today called "St. Paul's Bay." Just as Paul had prophesied, everyone escaped to land with their lives.[30]

---

30   When the people at Hawn's Mill sent Jacob Hawn to inquire of the Prophet what they should do—stay or flee to safety—Joseph Smith clearly told Jacob Hawn that the Saints at the mill should go to Far West for their own protection. Hawn feared losing his entire labor force, so he misrepresented Joseph Smith's counsel and told the Saints that the Prophet wanted them to stay if they could. When Joseph Smith heard of the massacre the next day—October 31—he was mortified that Jacob Hawn had not told the Saints that he wanted them to leave Hawn's Mill and go to Far West. The Prophet wrote, "Up to this day God had given me wisdom to save the people who took counsel. None had ever been killed who abode by my counsel." He added that innocent lives could have been preserved at Hawn's Mill had his counsel been received and followed. So it wasn't the fault of the Saints who didn't hearken to the counsel of Joseph Smith— they never GOT the counsel of Joseph Smith because Hawn didn't want them to leave. I fear that this paragraph casts unfair aspersions on the Saints, who thought they were obeying what they thought the Prophet had counseled. (Insight provided by Kathryn Jenkins.)

ACTS 28 AND CONCLUSION

Once on land, the inhabitants (called "barbarous," which means non-Greek or Latin speakers) received the shipwrecked passengers with many kindnesses, such as warming them with a fire. While gathering sticks to stoke the fire, Paul was bitten by a viper. The superstitious inhabitants believed that this was a sign of a murderer. Yet when Paul's hand did not swell and he did not fall ill or die, they instead hailed him as a god. We do not know how Paul reacted to such "honors," but Luke's text makes clear that Paul did much good among the people during the three months of wintry passage he spent on the island before the Rome-bound passengers were able to board a shipping vessel from Alexandria.

As we follow Paul's journey through the end of Acts, we learn that he had a private home in Rome where for two years he preached and received guests. Though it is traditionally assumed that Paul became a martyr for the Christian cause in Rome, Luke says nothing of the matter. In fact, and most remarkably, Luke closes his two-volume testimony of the origins and growth of Christianity (Luke through Acts) focused on Paul preaching the revealed gospel kingdom with much success:

> And Paul dwelt two whole years in his own hired house, and received all that came in unto him,
> Preaching the kingdom of God, and teaching those things which concern the Lord Jesus Christ, with all confidence, no man forbidding him. (Acts 28:30–31)

Luke closes Acts in this way with the hope that readers will look forward with faith—not to the suffering that may happen in this life, but to the sureties of joy to be had for all who accept Christ in their lives.

USING BIBLES TO STUDY PAUL

REGARDING THE STUDY OF PAUL, there are three important points to make. First, everyone should read Paul. Second, everyone should use more than one translation when reading Paul. Third, it's important to shed light on the work of biblical scholars, such as those who completed the King James Translation and all who labor to make the Bible more accessible and more understandable. The Bible is worthless if it is inaccessible or incomprehensible.

First, why should we read Paul? The most obvious reason is that more than half of the New Testament is attributed to him. More importantly, Paul is probably the most formative figure in establishing and expounding the doctrines of Christianity after the death of Christ. If Paul is the author of such a vast body of inestimably important material on Christ and Christianity, we should study him and his words as an additional witness of the mission and ministry of Christ.

Second, why should we use more than one translation when reading Paul? Once we are motivated to study the words of such an important Apostle, we must overcome the obstacles that hinder our understanding of Paul. Some of the obstacles are of our own making; they are in our own mind. We fear reading Paul (perhaps the same way in which we fear reading Isaiah), so we don't do it—and as a result, we lose the opportunity to understand this key witness of Christ.

Our fears concerning Paul are not without reason. We must be in good company when even Peter, the venerated Apostle, admitted in one of his epistles that Paul can be hard to understand:

So also our beloved brother Paul wrote to you according
to the wisdom given him, speaking of this as he does in all his
letters.

There are some things in them hard to understand. (2 Peter
3:15–16; NRSV translation)

Having admitted the real challenges that Paul's writing can pose, let's
consider how our comprehension can be magnified and enhanced.

Perhaps one of the best ways to understand Paul is to use the synoptic
method. We are all familiar with this approach as applied to the four
Gospels. They are called the "synoptic Gospels" because each offers a
unique view and testimony on the mission of Jesus Christ.[31] In other
words, each synoptic perspective offers information and insights that may
not be expressed by other witnesses. Each perspective plays a crucial role
in informing the whole.

Who among us does not benefit from a second opinion, from a
different viewpoint, from another way of seeing something? The synoptic
viewpoint is a way of seeing together through a chorus of harmonious
witnesses. And what better example of harmonious witnesses do we have
than the synoptic Gospels themselves? They offer unique access into
the powerful doctrines taught by the Master Teacher. Through these
accounts, we learn of His miraculous birth, His unparalleled mission, and
His all-encompassing charity of everlasting kindness known the world
over as the Atonement.

Let's consider the concept of the synoptic perspective from another
angle and see how such an approach to the Bible, especially to the
Pauline epistles, can enhance our insight and understanding. Let's apply
this concept to Bible translations (or "versions" if you will). Just as our
insight and understanding have been greatly enhanced through the
"seeing together" offered to us by the synoptic Gospels, so too can our
insight and understanding be enhanced by reading various translations of
the Bible. That also applies, of course, to the Pauline writings as well.

---

[31] Technically, only Matthew, Mark, and Luke are synoptic Gospels because of their
overabundant literary connections to each other, but for simplicity sake in this chapter
I include the Gospel as John as well, even though the Gospel of John is quite distinct
from the other three Gospels.

There are literally hundreds of available English translations of the Bible. Our King James Version (KJV) is one example. Other prominent examples include the following:

The New Jerusalem Bible (NJB)
The New King James Version (NKJV)
The New International Version (NIV)
The New American Bible (NAB)
The New Revised Standard Version (NRSV)

As you can see, many of these Bible translations have "new" in their name. This suggests that as our understanding of biblical texts and biblical languages improves, there is a need to update our Bible translations.

Now the task of translating the Bible is an extremely arduous one. What goes into such an effort? The answer sheds light on the work of biblical scholars who labor to make the Bible more accessible and more understandable.

Translating the Bible is a truly monumental effort. First, translators must review and analyze all available ancient documents and versions of the Old and New Testament. There are literally thousands of ancient documents that contain portions of the Old and/or New Testament, and variations of text and composition number in the tens of thousands! Scholars carefully examine each version, each text, each verse, and sometimes even the very letters of each word to determine which texts are most authentic and most reliable. Just as a detective seeks for the best evidence to make a case and rejects that which is unreliable, so too the biblical scholars work tediously and carefully to determine which ancient manuscripts are most authentic to the original authors.

Once the most reliable ancient Old and New Testament texts have been identified, scholars then begin the careful process of translating the texts into the target language (in this case, English) in a form that is both readable and understandable. This requires a thorough understanding of Hebrew and Aramaic (in order to translate the Old Testament) and Greek (in order to translate the New Testament. .

Do the translators slavishly stick to literal translation? Of course not; that would be impossible because of the nuances of words and grammar that do not easily cross over cultural barriers. As an example of how this works, consider why foreign diplomacy often fails. Sometimes words can have multiple meanings depending on context. In this case, the scholars seek to understand the meaning and intent of the passage as a whole, or they appeal to what we know about ancient cultures or customs of those times to make an appropriate translation. Each translation is reviewed many times by many people, not only to ensure accuracy but to achieve consensus among experts. The process is tedious, time-consuming, and usually does not offer very lucrative financial rewards.

Why, then, would anyone labor so intensely on such a project? If it's not financial, what *is* the reward? In most cases, these translators are people who care deeply about the Bible and its power to inform and enhance our lives. They strive to make the Bible both available and understandable to all people through translations. These translators and scholars realize that most people will not take the many years necessary to learn several dozen ancient languages and to master some four thousand years of history in order to gain access to the meaning of the texts in their original languages and contexts.

While most biblical scholars are God-fearing and well-intentioned people, they can't help but leave their "fingerprints" on the final product. It's an inescapable fact that every new translation of the Bible is essentially a "new version" that reflects the attitudes, values, and ideals of the time period in which it was translated. For example, the King James Version (KJV) reflects of seventeenth-century English culture—something most strongly reflected in the language and grammar used in the translation itself. After all, what other options did the translators have than to render the original Hebrew and Greek texts into the common tongue of their place and time?

That's exactly the point. Every time we translate the Bible, we cannot help but place our own fingerprints on the work. That does not necessarily mean that we have smudged the Bible or corrupted it; we should have no fear of translating and transmitting the Bible so that it continues to inform our spiritual lives today. In most cases today, new translations depend on the most ancient and authentic sources (usually Hebrew, Greek, and Aramaic) and not the translations of our own times. In other words, if I was attempting to translate the Bible into Spanish, I would not use the English KJV to do so. Such an approach would preserve the "fingerprints" of the King James translators into the Spanish version as well as adding the new "fingerprints" of Spanish culture and values embedded in the language of the translation. Rather it would be best to go back to the original languages of Hebrew, Greek, and Aramaic and make a fresh translation from those documents into Spanish. That way the intervening "fingerprints" of the KJV translators are not preserved and transmitted. This is not to sleight the KJV translators. What we are simply attempting to do is to get back to the most original and authentic versions of the biblical text.

It is important to realize that "fingerprints" come in various forms. Some translators seek to be "politically correct" in their translations. Other translations attempt to render the English in such a colloquial way as to make the Bible read as though it was the product of the lowest common denominator of meaning and vocabulary. As a result, no translation is without its deficiencies. Nevertheless, with some study, faith, prayer, and humility, supporting "synoptic" witnesses—especially Paul—can be selected to facilitate our reading of the Bible,

Here's one example of how reading a "synoptic" translation of Paul can enhance our study and understanding. Read both translations of 1 Corinthians 14:1–12 below and then ask yourself if this exercise increases your comprehension of Paul's explanation of the gifts of the Spirit. If it does, then you are already on your way to experiencing the value of using various translations in your study.

King James Version	New Revised Standard Version
Follow after charity, and desire spiritual *gifts*, but rather that ye may prophesy. 2 For he that speaketh in an unknown tongue speaketh not unto men, but unto God: for no man understandeth him; howbeit in the spirit he speaketh mysteries. 3 But he that prophesieth speaketh unto men to edification, and exhortation, and comfort. 4 He that speaketh in an unknown tongue edifieth himself; but he that prophesieth edifieth the church. 5 I would that ye all spake with tongues, but rather that ye prophesied: for greater is he that prophesieth than he that speaketh with tongues, except he interpret, that the church may receive edifying.	Pursue love and strive for the spiritual gifts, and especially that you may prophesy. 2 For those who speak in a tongue do not speak to other people but to God; for nobody understands them, since they are speaking mysteries in the Spirit. 3 On the other hand, those who prophesy speak to other people for their upbuilding and encouragement and consolation. 4 Those who speak in a tongue build up themselves, but those who prophesy build up the church. 5 Now I would like all of you to speak in tongues, but even more to prophesy. One who prophesies is greater than one who speaks in tongues, unless someone interprets, so that the church may be built up.

6 Now, brethren, if I come unto you speaking with tongues, what shall I profit you, except I shall speak to you either by revelation, or by knowledge, or by prophesying, or by doctrine?

7 And even things without life giving sound, whether pipe or harp, except they give a distinction in the sounds, how shall it be known what is piped or harped?

8 For if the trumpet give an uncertain sound, who shall prepare himself to the battle?

9 So likewise ye, except ye utter by the tongue words easy to be understood, how shall it be known what is spoken? for ye shall speak into the air.

10 There are, it may be, so many kinds of voices in the world, and none of them is without signification.

11 Therefore if I know not the meaning of the voice, I shall be unto him that speaketh a barbarian, and he that speaketh shall be a barbarian unto me.

12 Even so ye, forasmuch as ye are zealous of spiritual gifts, seek that ye may excel to the edifying of the church.

6 Now, brothers and sisters, if I come to you speaking in tongues, how will I benefit you unless I speak to you in some revelation or knowledge or prophecy or teaching?

7 It is the same way with lifeless instruments that produce sound, such as the flute or the harp. If they do not give distinct notes, how will anyone know what is being played?

8 And if the bugle gives an indistinct sound, who will get ready for battle?

9 So with yourselves; if in a tongue you utter speech that is not intelligible, how will anyone know what is being said? For you will be speaking into the air.

10 There are doubtless many different kinds of sounds in the world, and nothing is without sound.

11 If then I do not know the meaning of a sound, I will be a foreigner to the speaker and the speaker a foreigner to me.

12 So with yourselves; since you are eager for spiritual gifts, strive to excel in them for building up the church.

I hope this exercise gave you a taste of the value of using a variety of Bible translations to support and enlarge your engagement with the word of God. Learning is an act of God. Seeking to better understand His word can only bring greater peace, satisfaction, meaning, and purpose to our lives. I hope you continue to seek after great Biblical understanding by taking advantage of various fine Bible translations.

1 CORINTHIANS 11–16: UNITY IN CHRIST

"Let all things be done decently and in order."
—*1 Corinthians 14:40*

PAUL WROTE 1 CORINTHIANS TO help dispel the disorder and disunity disrupting the Corinthian church. As we study the final six chapters of Paul's first epistle to the Corinthians, the most important thing for us to understand is Paul's overriding purpose in writing the letter in the first place. Sometimes we become so excited by the doctrines and principles shared throughout the many passages that we miss the context and reason for their inclusion.

In short, Paul's original purpose in writing this epistle was to deal with division and general disorder among the early Christian Saints living in the city of Corinth. To avoid being too hasty in reprimanding these erring Saints, we need to realize that misunderstanding, disunity, disorder, and carelessness are the common lot of human experience. In other words, Paul's admonitions for unity and decency are as relevant in our day as they were in his day, though with some cultural nuances.

Remembering that the entire epistle is couched in Paul addressing the circumstances of increasing disorder, indecency, and disunity in the Corinthian branch of the early Church, we can turn our attention to specific doctrines and principles taught by Paul to overcome these problems.

1 CORINTHIANS 11—HAIRSTYLES AND POTLUCK DINNERS

Even ancient people had controversy over hairstyles and potluck dinners as we do today. Paul addresses the problems of hairstyles first in this chapter (see verses 1–16). Verse 6 is comparable to what Orthodox Jewish women do today. Once married, many shave their head and then wear a wig to avoid showing their hair to anyone but their husband.[32] Some of the women in Corinth were apparently wearing their hair in such a way at church that it was causing a general disturbance.

Paul uses several arguments to overcome this problem (see verses 3–15), some of which certainly related to the culture in Corinth. Perhaps today we would not use the same cultural measuring stick to judge if someone had a disruptive hairstyle. In that culture, however, the hairstyles worn at church were different enough to cause disturbance, impeding the work of the Lord.

What types of hairstyles were so egregious? Apparently, the way the hair was styled wasn't the only problem. Rather, the problem was the association particular hairstyles had with prostitution and licentiousness. In the days of Paul there was a Greek religion near Corinth that encouraged sexual liberty. The women who joined that religious movement and engaged in the associated licentious behavior wore their hair in a distinct fashion. Some of the women of the Corinthian Church apparently had similar hairstyles, which caused other members to question whether these Christian women were united to the licentious practices of a nearby Greek religion.

Paul addressed the issue by encouraging Church members not to wear hairstyles similar to those associated with perverse religions and beliefs. An analogy to this were the rules put in place at BYU in the 1970s to counteract the counter-culture movement of the 1960s and 1970s where many social dissidents defied mainstream culture by wearing long hair and beards. BYU did not participate much in such protests and essentially took a stand against such counter-culturalism by encouraging that those who came to BYU not dress or look like those who professed counter-culturalism. Nevertheless, we must always be careful; misjudgments are easy to make, and outward appearance (whether consisting of clothing, hair, or something else) is not always a reliable sign.

Paul then moved on in his epistle to address the confusion that reigned at the "ward dinner parties" at Corinth (see verses 17–34). Apparently, many members came to church early to eat dinner (as church

---

[32] This idea was provided by my wife, Lisa Maren Rampton Halverson.

meetings were likely held in the evening). Some began eating before others arrived for the meal. Still others came just for the church meetings and were hungry. As a result, hurt feelings, jealousies, anger, and division developed.

Paul, using the symbol of the sacrament, taught the Saints that they should all be alike in their common meals at church, just as all who are worthy can participate in the sacrament. He then urged the members to wait to eat together if they were going to have a "ward dinner party." Otherwise, he said, everyone should eat at home before church meetings in order to avoid having some members satiated while others went hungry.

1 CORINTHIANS 12—DIVERSITY OF GIFTS

After addressing the mundane issues of hairstyles and ward dinners, Paul moved to a more serious topic—spiritual gifts. We know from scripture that each individual is blessed with a gift of the Spirit. But knowing what we do about the Corinthian Saints—and, for that matter, what we know about human nature in general—we should not be surprised to learn that there was contention and competition over whose gifts were more beautiful, useful, necessary, and so on.

Paul taught that "there are diversities of gifts, *but the same Spirit*" (1 Corinthians 12:4, emphasis added). He acknowledged that everyone had a gift, but then he brought about unity by stressing that each gift comes from God through the Spirit. Paul then lists many of the spiritual gifts and explains how each gift is like a part of the body—each a portion of a larger whole that itself cannot fully function without each particular gift. As all members are part of one body, they should rejoice and suffer together, not contend with each other over the value of their gifts.

Alma the Elder taught this same principle to the Saints who gathered at the Waters of Mormon:

> Behold, here are the waters of Mormon (for thus were they called) and now, as ye are desirous to come into the fold of God, and to be called his people, and are willing to bear one another's burdens, that they may be light;
>
> Yea, and are willing to mourn with those that mourn; yea, and comfort those that stand in need of comfort, and to stand as

witnesses of God at all times and in all things, and in all places
that ye may be in, even until death, that ye may be redeemed of
God, and be numbered with those of the first resurrection, that ye
may have eternal life—

Now I say unto you, if this be the desire of your hearts, what
have you against being baptized in the name of the Lord, as a
witness before him that ye have entered into a covenant with him,
that ye will serve him and keep his commandments, that he may
pour out his Spirit more abundantly upon you?

And now when the people had heard these words, they
clapped their hands for joy, and exclaimed [in unity]: This is the
desire of our hearts. (Mosiah 18:8–11)

Thus as one body we are to rejoice and suffer together, for it is our
covenant, and together we are to share and reap the blessings of the
multitude of spiritual gifts. In closing his chapter, Paul encourages the
Saints to seek after these best gifts, and then he promises to show them a
more excellent way. 1 Corinthians 13 reveals that more excellent way.

1 CORINTHIANS 13—CHARITY, A MORE EXCELLENT WAY

After the discussion of various gifts of the Spirit and their
administration and uses, Paul lifts the sights of Christians with a beautiful
reminder that all the gifts of the Spirit are nothing in comparison to the
gift of charity:

Though I speak with the tongues of men and of angels, and have
not charity, I am become *as* sounding brass, or a tinkling cymbal.

And though I have the gift of prophecy, and understand all
mysteries, and all knowledge; and though I have all faith, so that I
could remove mountains, and have not charity, I am nothing.

And though I bestow all my goods to feed the poor, and
though I give my body to be burned, and have not charity, it
profiteth me nothing.

Charity suffereth long, and is kind; charity envieth not;
charity vaunteth not itself, is not puffed up,

Doth not behave itself unseemly, seeketh not her own, is not
easily provoked, thinketh no evil;

Rejoiceth not in iniquity, but rejoiceth in the truth;

Beareth all things, believeth all things, hopeth all things, endureth all things.

Charity never faileth: but whether there be prophecies, they shall fail; whether there be tongues, they shall cease; whether there be knowledge, it shall vanish away.

For we know in part, and we prophesy in part.

But when that which is perfect is come, then that which is in part shall be done away.

When I was a child, I spake as a child, I understood as a child, I thought as a child: but when I became a man, I put away childish things.

For now we see through a glass, darkly; but then face to face: now I know in part; but then shall I know even as also I am known.

And now abideth faith, hope, charity, these three; but the greatest of these *is* charity. (1 Corinthians 13:1–13)

What is charity, then? To enhance our understanding, let's search the Old Testament. The underlying Hebrew word for charity is *hesed*. It is a word rich in beautiful meaning, for it refers to loving kindness, loyalty, steadfastness, everlasting love, mercy, and the bonds of covenant fidelity. Just as God will be forever loyal and faithful to the covenants He has made with us, we too should be loyal and faithful to Him. Indeed, it is in the bonds of covenant relationships that true and pure *hesed* can be lived and experienced.

Turning to the New Testament, we find that *charity* is translated from the Greek word *xaris* (*charis*). Before we look at the definition of that Greek word, it is significant to note that the English words *charity* and *grace* both derive from the Greek word *xaris*. It means to have favor, good will, love, mercy, and compassion on another. Interestingly, this word is often used to describe the loving mercy and compassion given to those who do not deserve such acts. In this respect, the ultimate example of *xaris*/charity/grace is God, for none of us could ever be deserving of His boundless loving kindness on our own. It is only through His *xaris* or grace that we are healed from the effects of a broken law. And so God indeed is the fullness of *xaris*/charity.

Xaris is also used to describe the presence of God and His glory. Knowing that, the following verse takes on new meaning, for when we are filled with charity we are most like God and most ready to "see him as he is."

> Wherefore, my beloved brethren, pray unto the Father with all the energy of heart, that ye may be filled with this love, which he hath bestowed upon all who are true followers of his Son, Jesus Christ; that ye may become the sons of God; that when he shall appear we shall be like him, for we shall see him as he is; that we may have this hope; that we may be purified even as he is pure. (Moroni 7:48)

1 CORINTHIANS 14—ADMINISTERING SPIRITUAL GIFTS

After taking some moments to explain the power of the gift of charity, Paul returned to setting the Church in Corinth to order and peace, particularly on the subject of gifts of the Spirit. He had already singled out charity as the greatest of any gift, but now he wished to describe the use and function of other gifts. His focus here was on the gifts of prophecy and the gift of speaking in and interpreting tongues.

The academic term used to talk about speaking in tongues is *glossolalia*. The Greek word *gloss* means "tongue." Again, if we study this chapter in the context of Paul's desire to put order and decency back into a church where there had been misunderstanding and much disorder, this whole chapter makes much more sense.

First, Paul teaches the difference between the gift of prophecy and the gift of tongues. The gift of prophecy is for edifying the whole congregation, while the gift of tongues is just for edifying oneself. Paul then explains that if there is an individual in the congregation who has the gift of interpreting tongues and can interpret what was said by the person who has the gift of tongues, then the whole congregation can be edified by the gift of speaking in tongues.

Paul issues cautions regarding these gifts. They are to be used in turn—that is, everyone is not to speak at once. Additionally, the gift of speaking in tongues should be used in public only if there is in the audience an individual who has the gift to interpret tongues. And finally, if many people have the gift of prophecy, they should not all speak and prophesy at once, for then what was intended to edify the entire group will be lost in the clamor and turmoil of competing voices.

In summary, Paul exhorts the Corinthian Saints to (1) use all gifts to edify, (2) prophesy one by one, that all may learn and all may be comforted and encouraged, and (3) let all things be done decently and in order (see 1 Corinthians 14:26, 31, 40).

1 CORINTHIANS 15—PREACHING THE DOCTRINE OF RESURRECTION

Having dealt with much of the disunity affecting the Corinthians Saints, Paul took the opportunity to expound on the doctrine of resurrection. Being young in the gospel, some of these Saints needed additional light and knowledge on this important gospel principle, because they had questioned whether the resurrection was real (see 1 Corinthians 15:12).

With the most powerful evidence he could muster, Paul testified of the reality of resurrection through his witness that Christ the Lord was resurrected. Paul appealed to the numerous witnesses (more than five hundred in number) who had seen the resurrected Lord with their own eyes. Then with a clarity and force of thought, Paul reasoned with the Saints:

> But if there be no resurrection of the dead, then is Christ not risen:
>
> And if Christ be not risen, then is our preaching vain, and your faith is also vain.
>
> Yea, and we are found false witnesses of God; because we have testified of God that he raised up Christ: whom he raised not up, if so be that the dead rise not.
>
> For if the dead rise not, then is not Christ raised:
>
> And if Christ be not raised, your faith is vain; ye are yet in your sins.
>
> Then they also which are fallen asleep in Christ are perished.
>
> If in this life only we have hope in Christ, we are of all men most miserable.

But now is Christ risen from the dead, and become the firstfruits of them that slept.

For since by man came death, by man came also the resurrection of the dead.

For as in Adam all die, even so in Christ shall all be made alive. (1 Corinthians 15:13–22)

This theological reasoning is similar to Lehi's powerful theology on the existence of God, the reality of the plan of happiness, and the nature of agency, righteousness, and happiness (see 2 Nephi 2).

Paul then offered additional proof of the reality of resurrection by an additional logical argument. Appealing to a well-known practice in the Christian church at that time, Paul queried the Saints, "What shall they do which are baptized for the dead, if the dead rise not at all? why are they then baptized for the dead?" (1 Corinthians 15:29). In other words, if there is no such thing as the resurrection, why in the world are we spending our time with the work of redeeming the dead?

Paul continued to answer those who doubted in the resurrection. Not being resurrected would simply involve a life of eating and drinking and making merry, for tomorrow we die and there would be nothing of concern after death (see also 2 Nephi 28:7–8).

Some Saints were apparently worried about *how* they would be resurrected. In response, Paul taught the principle that whatever one sows is what one will reap. Alma the Younger taught similar principles to his wayward and questioning son Corianton on this same subject (see especially Alma 40–41):

It is requisite with the justice of God that men should be judged according to their works; and if their works were good in this life, and the desires of their hearts were good, that they should also, at the last day, be restored unto that which is good.

And if their works are evil they shall be restored unto them for evil. Therefore, all things shall be restored to their proper order, every thing to its natural frame—mortality raised to immortality, corruption to incorruption—raised to endless happiness to inherit the kingdom of God, or to endless misery to inherit the kingdom of the devil, the one on one hand, the other on the other—

The one raised to happiness according to his desires of happiness, or good according to his desires of good; and the other to evil according to his desires of evil; for as he has desired to do evil all the day long even so shall he have his reward of evil when the night cometh.

And so it is on the other hand. If he hath repented of his sins, and desired righteousness until the end of his days, even so he shall be rewarded unto righteousness. (Alma 41:3–6)

One of the most important principles Paul taught concerning the resurrection, and one that was echoed by Alma as we see above, is the idea that just as there are many states of righteousness here on earth, so too there will be various manifestations of resurrected beings in the next life, according to their righteousness. Some will be resurrected into celestial glory, others into terrestrial glory, and some into telestial glory.

After testifying so boldly of the reality of resurrection and the necessity of righteousness in this life if we are to receive a brilliant resurrection into the next, Paul left a final admonition for his beloved Saints in Corinth concerning this topic: "Therefore, my beloved brethren, be ye steadfast, unmoveable, always abounding in the work of the Lord, forasmuch as ye know that your labour is not in vain in the Lord" (1 Corinthians 15:58).

1 CORINTHIANS 16—EPISTOLARY FAREWELL

Our understanding of this particular chapter is enhanced once we understand letter writing and letter formats of the ancient New Testament world. The material in this chapter comes from an epistle or letter. Just as the First Presidency may send out a letter today to all bishops to be read over the pulpit in sacrament meeting, so too Paul wrote a letter that was to be read to all the Saints in Corinth. And just as there is a customary introduction and closing in the First Presidency letters of today (such as "Dear Brothers and Sisters" and "Your Brethren in the Lord"), so too in Paul's day there were customary ways to begin and end a letter.

Of course, what we have here as written by Paul is deemed scripture. The formal closing of a First Presidency letter, though it is from the First Presidency, usually doesn't have the same weighty substance as the main body of the letter. That same thing applies to Paul's epistles.

What we have in 1 Corinthians 16 is Paul's formal close to his letter. It is full of blessings and reminders to greet friends and associates. These are all interesting highlights about the culture and activities of the people in that day, and every now and then there is a gospel principle or exhortation placed in the closing statements. When we recognize these closing statements (such as 1 Corinthians 16) as the formal close to a letter, we can begin to appreciate the purpose and meaning behind these types of verses and chapters found in our scriptures.

CONCLUSION

What an immense blessing and miracle it is that the words of the Apostle Paul have been preserved and transmitted to us through the many centuries since his day. Just think of the effort, the time, and the care required to painstakingly and meticulously copy these words over and over so they might be available to readers eager for the truth. And what a blessing it is that we have principles and doctrines that can speak to our day and time.

The Saints of Corinth needed direction and encouragement, and sometimes practical advice, to ply the seemingly unchartered waters of life; we can take strength from the experiences and doctrines that guided their community. Thus we can apply these things to ourselves. Are we the cause of any disunity in our families, wards, or stakes? Are we promoting lifestyles that are contrary to the principles of order and happiness? Do we hear with eager humility the voice of God through the scriptures and living witnesses? Whatever our personal weaknesses and challenges, the persistent invitation from the Savior is before us: "Come unto me, all ye that labour and are heavy laden, and I will give you rest. Take my yoke upon you, and learn of me; for I am meek and lowly in heart: and ye shall find rest unto your souls. For my yoke is easy, and my burden is light" (Matthew 11:28–19).

We have covenanted to build Zion, so we should strive to overcome disunity, misunderstanding, and division. By so doing we can indeed play a positive role in building Zion upon the earth, the city beautiful where all hearts are knit into one: "And the Lord called his people ZION, because they were of one heart and one mind, and dwelt in righteousness" (Moses 8:18).

JAMES: EXHORT AND ENCOURAGE

JAMES MAY BE THE MOST important book of scripture for the Restoration. The now-famous passage, "If any of you lack wisdom, let him ask of God" (James 1:5), inspired the young Joseph Smith to ponder deeply, which in turn led him to follow the simple and pragmatic counsel to inquire of the Lord.

This straightforward, pragmatic approach has long been a noted feature of James, who focused his short epistle on the practical actions and works of the gospel in contrast to the Pauline writings that lay much emphasis on justification through faith.

AUTHORSHIP

Who wrote the epistle of James? The seemingly obvious answer would be James. But which James? Six men named James are referred to throughout the New Testament, which can be rather confusing and can legitimately cause us to wonder who wrote this epistle.

Many believe that James, the brother of Jesus, authored this epistle. There are two main reasons for this belief. First are the similarities between the teachings of James the brother of Jesus in Acts 15 and those in the epistle of James. The second is that James, the brother of Jesus, is the most prominent among the men named James who are mentioned in the New Testament; as such, his first name would be the only introduction he needed.

As one biblical scholar wrote,

> The New Testament mentions a number of persons named James: the son of Zebedee (Mark 1:19), the son of Alphaeus (Mark 3:18), the brother of Jesus (Mark 6:3), James, the younger

(Mark 15:40), and James, the father of Jude (Luke 6:16). Of that group, only James, the son of Zebedee, and James, the brother of the Lord, could be described as well-known figures. Acts 12:1–2 indicates that James, the son of Zebedee, was martyred by Agrippa I (d. 44 C.E.). Since Paul indicates that James, the brother of the Lord, was one of the leaders in Jerusalem along with Peter and John (Gal. 2:1–14), James, the brother of the Lord, appears to be the individual referred to as the sender of the letter.[33]

SETTING AND AUDIENCE

James does not date his document and tells us very little about the immediate intended audience to which he is writing. He simply states in 1:1 that he is writing "to the twelve tribes which are scattered abroad," though in 2:2 we know that his audience assembled at a synagogue that was led by elders (see James 5:14).

Some have speculated that the strong themes of social justice—such as mercy and compassion for the suffering innocent and poor—may reflect the very social situations among many Jewish Christians in and around Jerusalem around 50 AD. Acts 6 described that some widows were being neglected in the daily ministration of support and sustenance in the Church. Additionally, the economic standing of many (including the Christians) in Palestine during the middle decades of the first century AD was quite oppressive and restrictive. Those who had money and especially those who had Roman citizenship were given many favors, while those who did not were considered second-class citizens at best. In most cases these poor lacked any power to protect themselves from the rich who lived off their labors, misfortunes, and weaknesses. So perhaps this document was written in that type of environment.

STYLE

The epistle of James is remarkable for the exhortation style that dominates the entire document. Of the 108 verses of James, 54 of them—exactly half—use imperative/command forms of verbs. Such strong words can stir the heart of even the most hardened hearer to do the works of righteousness. Examples

---

[33] Pheme Perkins, *First and Second Peter, James, and Jude* in the series *Interpretation: A Bible Commentary for Teaching and Preaching*, James Luther, Patrick Miller, Jr., and Paul Achtemeier, eds. (Louisville, KY: John Knox Press, 1995), 83.

of the exhortation style James employs using command forms include "submit yourselves," "resist the devil," "draw nigh unto God," "cleanse your hands," and "purify your hearts" (see James 4:7–8).

THEMES IN THE EPISTLE OF JAMES

Doers of the Word

One of the most striking features of the epistle of James is the stance, "But be ye doers of the word and not hearers only, deceiving your own selves" (James 1:22). James powerfully elaborates this pragmatic, simple wisdom in James 2, explaining, "Even so faith, it if have not works, is dead, being alone. Therefore wilt thou know, O vain man, that faith without works is dead and cannot save you?" (JST James 2:17–18). And in case any misunderstand how this principle is applied, James provides ready and penetrating examples:

Example 1 (James 2:1–4; NRSV translation)

My brothers and sisters, do you with your acts of favoritism really believe in our glorious Lord Jesus Christ? For if a person with gold rings and in fine clothes comes into your assembly, and if a poor person in dirty clothes also comes in, and if you take notice of the one wearing the fine clothes and say, "Have a seat here, please," while to the one who is poor you say, "Stand there," or, "Sit at my feet," have you not made distinctions among yourselves, and become judges with evil thoughts?

Example 2 (James 2:8–11; NRSV translation)

You do well if you really fulfill the royal law according to the scripture, "You shall love your neighbor as yourself." But if you show partiality, you commit sin and are convicted by the law as transgressors. For whoever keeps the whole law but fails in one point has become accountable for all of it. For the one who said, "You shall not commit adultery," also said, "You shall not murder." Now if you do not commit adultery but if you murder, you have become a transgressor of the law.

Example 3 (James 2:14–16; JST)

What profit is it, my brethren, for a man to say he hath faith, and hath not works? can faith save him? Yea, a man may say, I will show thee

I have faith without works; but I say, Show me thy faith without works, and I will show thee my faith by my works. For if a brother or sister be naked and destitute, and one of you say, Depart in peace, be warmed and filled; notwithstanding he give not those things which are needful to the body; what profit is your faith unto such?

Prayer

James commends the worshipful practice of prayer throughout his epistle. If we need knowledge or wisdom, we can use prayer to seek the very source of all truth. James testifies that those who petition God with confidence and faith will be richly rewarded (see James 1:5). The story of Joseph Smith is a strong witness for this promise.

If one is sick, James reminds the Saints to pray, promising that "the prayer of the faith shall save the sick; and the Lord shall raise him up; and if he have committed sins, they shall be forgiven him" (James 5:15). If there is sin among the Saints, James again encourages prayer for healing and reconciliation, teaching the Saints to "confess your faults one to another, and pray one for another, that ye may be healed. The effectual fervent prayer of a righteous man availeth much" (James 5:16). To underscore this principle, James cites the story of Elijah, the righteous Old Testament prophet who prayed to God on behalf of Israel to cause the rain to fall again upon the land after three and a half years of famine.

Rich and Poor

James has very strong things to say against the rich. Each of us can look deeply at our own lives and query whether these words describe us (see especially James 2:1–10; 5:1–6). His tone toward the poor, on the other hand, is most merciful and promissory comparable to what we hear from Christ at the Sermon on the Mount:

Sermon on the Mount	Epistle of James
"Blessed are the poor…for theirs is the kingdom of heaven…blessed are the meek for they shall inherit the earth" (Matthew 5:3, 5)	"Let the brother of low degree rejoice in that he is exalted." (James 1:9) "Hearken, my beloved brethren, Hath not God chosen the poor of this world rich in faith, and heirs of kingdom which he hath promised to them that love him?" (James 2:5)

Suffering of the Innocent

Suffering is a fact of mortality and has been a persistent literary theme for millennia. Where does suffering come from? Our own choices can cause us to suffer, as can the choices of others. Ultimately, we alone are responsible for how we deal with suffering, regardless of whether it is self-inflicted or caused by others.

Suffering is very real, and is acutely real for those who innocently struggle under various forms of oppression and injustice. To these individuals, James writes comfortingly:

Be patient therefore, brethren, unto the coming of the Lord. Behold, the husbandman waiteth for the precious fruit of the earth, and hath long patience for it, until he receive the early and latter rain.

Be ye also patient; stablish your hearts; for the coming of the Lord draweth nigh.

Grudge not one against another, brethren, lest ye be condemned; behold, the judge standeth before the door.

Take, my brethren, the prophets, who have spoken in the name of the Lord, for an example of suffering affliction, and of patience.

Behold, we count them happy which endure. Ye have heard of the patience of Job, and have seen the end of the Lord; that the Lord is very pitiful, and of tender mercy. (James 5:7–11)

Bridling Our Tongues

We all know the evils of gossip, false accusations, lies, deceit, and unkind remarks. James's pragmatic, yet exceedingly sharp gospel perspective is quite evident in his exhortations against the follies of a loose tongue:

> The tongue is a small member, yet it boasts of great exploits. How great a forest is set ablaze by a small fire!....But no one can tame the tongue—a restless evil, full of deadly poison. With it we bless the Lord and Father, and with it we curse those who are made in the likeness of God. From the same mouth come blessing and cursing. My brothers and sisters, this ought not to be so. Does a spring pour forth from the same opening both fresh and brackish water? (James 3:5, 8–11; NRSV translation)

If we control our tongues, James makes a most astounding promise to us: "If any man offend not in word, the same is a perfect man, and able also to bridle the whole body" (James 3:2). Do we believe it? Do we have enough faith to test the word? Imagine the payoff of such a promise! If we can bridle our tongue, we will then have power over all other passions and desires that seek to dominate our soul: "Wherefore, my beloved brethren, let every man be swift to hear, slow to speak, slow to wrath" (James 1:19).

Social Justice

"Now, what do we hear in the gospel which we have received? A voice of gladness! A voice of mercy from heaven; and a voice of truth out of the earth" (D&C 128:19). The gladness of the gospel is but tinkling cymbals and sounding brass if we neglect the poor, the naked, the hungry, the widow, the fatherless, the friendless, the oppressed, and the forsaken. "Pure religion and undefiled before God and the Father is this, To visit the fatherless and widows in their affliction, and to keep [yourself] unspotted from the world" (James 1:27).

In this regard, no amount of faith can ever compensate for the living realities of unattended suffering unless it is coupled with the power of action. James explains this with vivid clarity:

What doth it profit, my brethren, though a man say he hath faith, and have not works? Can faith save him?

If a brother or sister be naked, and destitute of daily food,

And one of you say unto them, Depart in peace, be ye warmed and filled; notwithstanding ye give them not those things which are needful to the body; what doth it profit?

Even so faith, if it hath not works, is dead, being alone.

Yea, a man may say, Thou hast faith, and I have works: shew me thy faith without thy works, and I will shew thee my faith by my works. (James 2:14–18)

Following the exhortation of James, let us press forward in the faith of righteous works, attending to the needs, distresses, and suffering of those children of God all around us.

REVELATION 5–6 AND 19–22: VIEWS AND PERSPECTIVES

INTRODUCTION

THE BOOK OF REVELATION HAS long been the source of much mystery, speculation, fantastic interpretations, and the near-suffocating fervor that the world will be destroyed in five minutes. Though the book of Revelation can cause confusion because of its bizarre images, strange symbols, and unfamiliar sights, we can take courage that with some simple interpretive keys the words, symbols, and messages of this text can have great meaning for our lives today.

Joseph Smith encouraged us with the words, "The Book of Revelation is one of the plainest books God ever caused to be written."[34] If we exercise our faith and go to work reading, thinking, and praying about the text, we will discover, as Joseph Smith declared, that the book of Revelation is indeed quite plain. Again, this takes faith and work.

With this in mind, we'll briefly review some interpretive methods used over the centuries to understand Revelation. Next we will turn to Nephi for interpretive guidance. Finally, we will discuss the broader themes evident in chapters 5–6 and 19–22 as John saw them.

INTERPRETIVE APPROACHES[35]

Several interpretive approaches have been used in the past two thousand years to understand the book of Revelation. While I am not necessarily advocating the use of these interpretive approaches, I offer them to show the wide range of differing voices and perspectives on the same text.

---

[34] *History of the Church*, 5:342.
[35] Adapted from John M. Court, *Myth and History in the Book of Revelation* (Atlanta: John Knox Press, 1979).

Chiliastic Interpretation

This term derives from the Greek word for the number 1000, or millennium. The word *millennium* derives from two Latin words that together mean "1000 years" (*mil* meaning 1000, and *annum* meaning year). Using this approach, some ancient writers and commentators interpret the book of Revelation as speaking about the events leading up to and constituting the Millennium.

Allegorical Interpretation

Other interpreters have looked at the book of Revelation from an allegorical standpoint. They believe that everything in the text is to be read as symbolizing other things and that the book is not to be read literally.

Recapitulation Interpretation

This interpretive method believes "that [the book of Revelation] is not a strictly consecutive [or chronological] account of a sequence of events, but a description which repeats the same facts in different forms, such as the seven seals, trumpets and bowls."[36]

Historical Application Interpretation

Many Medieval commentators believed that the book of Revelation revealed the stages of world history or church history. Using what was contained in the book of Revelation, interpreters over hundreds of years believed they were living in the final stage of world history. Each generation believed that the final stage of Revelation referred to their own day and that they were living in the last days.

Eschatological Interpretations

The term *eschaton* is a Greek word that means "end, last, final"; the term *eschatological* means "the things of the last days, the end times." The eschatological approach usually has reference to a great confusion and disorder, both in nature and society, that immediately proceeds the passing away of one age and the inauguration of a new age of peace and justice. This interpretive method is similar to the *chiliastic* approach described above, but it focuses more on the confusion, persecutions,

---

[36] Court, 5.

injustices, and wickedness of the last days that are then overturned by the righteous acts of God, placing everything into order again.

Contemporary Historical Interpretations

This method was invented with the rise of modern biblical scholarship (starting in the seventeenth century). It seeks to interpret the book of Revelation through the events contemporary with its ancient author. Scholars have studied the society and history of the time of the author to inform their reading and understanding of Revelation; this included a study of the Greco-Roman and Jewish social environments in which John lived. Such an approach is like taking the Gettysburg address and reading it not just as a beautiful prayer, but seeking to understand the Civil War and the historical circumstance from which the address emerged.

Literary Analysis Interpretation

This approach believes that we can best understand a text by knowing the type of text it is. For example, one would not read a business report as a fairy tale. Expressed in another way, if I know that the story I am about to read is a fairy tale, I already know certain things about such stories, and thus I have certain expectations from the text—things like a plot, some suspense, and a happy ending.

In a similar way, scholars have sifted through the enormous amount of ancient literature available to us to find other writings that are similar to the book of Revelation. In so doing they have hoped to find clues and insights as to how to read the book. The book of Daniel is an example of literature that relates in literary form to the book of Revelation: as just one example, a prophet sees a vision and is then guided by an angel, who explains and interprets the vision. For many years scholars have increased our understanding of both Daniel and Revelation by reading them as similar texts.

Comparative Studies Interpretation

This approach, which borrows from the contemporary historical interpretation and literary analysis interpretation methods, seeks to understand how the symbols, ideas, and imagery used by an author may have been used or understood in the larger society within which the author lived. For example, if I use a red light to symbolize caution or danger, someone could study the larger society around me and discover that my use of a red light is not unique, but rather is well known and understood throughout society. However, if I used a red light to symbolize a cool glass of water on a hot day, someone studying my larger society would probably determine that I used a common symbol in a new and inventive, if not a strange, way.

NEPHI'S INTERPRETATION

There is not one single way to read, interpret, and find meaning in the scriptures. However, some methods are better than others. For example, interpretive methods found throughout other passages of our canon or the methods used by authorized Church leaders can offer us rewarding and meaningful insights into these texts. Nephi is a good example.

Let's look at the interpretive keys Nephi's record offers us for understanding the book of Revelation. Like John the Revelator, Nephi received a powerful vision of many events in world history. These are recorded in 1 Nephi 11–14. At the end of Nephi's visionary account, the Lord showed him John the Revelator and explained:

> And behold, the things which this apostle of the Lamb shall write are many things which thou hast seen; and behold, the remainder shalt thou see.
> But the things which thou shalt see hereafter thou shalt not write; for the Lord God hath ordained the apostle of the lamb of God that he should write them. (1 Nephi 14:24–25)

Herein the Lord explicitly forbade Nephi from recording everything he saw, yet promised that a record would be made by John the Apostle, who would see the same things. What are those things that John was to record? "Behold, he [John] shall see and write the remainder of these things; yea, and also many things which have been. And he shall also write concerning the end of the world" (1 Nephi 14:21–22).

1 Nephi 14 also preserves for us crucial information about the composition of the book of Revelation.

Wherefore, the things which he shall write are just and true; and behold they are written in the book which thou beheld proceeding out of the mouth of the Jew; and at the time they proceeded out of the mouth of the Jew, or, at the time the book proceeded out of the mouth of the Jew, the things which were written were plain and pure, and most precious and easy to the understanding of all men (1 Nephi 14:23).

This passage of scripture may be the reason that Joseph Smith said, "The book of Revelation is one of the plainest books God ever caused to be written." In the Prophet's defense, it may be that at the time when John wrote the book of Revelation it was plain and easy to understand but that over the years the text was modified so its plainness was compromised.

In summary, we learn through Nephi that John the Revelator saw many things concerning the history of the world and the end of the world, that John was commissioned to write about the things of the last days, and that when John completed his writing it was plain and easy to understand.

READING REVELATION

When I read Revelation (which is only one approach for gaining meaning from the text), I think in several broad themes to help me understand the "drama" that is occurring. First, Satan attacks the work of God and the Saints of God. Second, the suffering righteous endure through faith until the end. Third, the Lord comes triumphant to the destruction of the forces of evil and to the justification and sanctification of the Saints. And fourth, there is final peace and joy of the righteous with God in the New Jerusalem on earth. With that, let's look at the text of Revelation 5–6 and 19–22.

REVELATION 5–6

This discussion starts in the middle of John's revelation/vision; it is as though we have walked into a theater performance twenty minutes after opening. So let's get up to speed with what is happening.

John is witnessing a vision of heaven, partially accompanied by an angelic guide (just as Nephi was accompanied in his grand vision). In

Revelation 4, John had seen and begun to describe his vision of the heavenly realms and God's throne. As Revelation 5 begins, he sees a book in the right hand of God that was bound and sealed with seven rings; no one could open it. Each seal represented things pertaining to a set of one thousand years (see D&C 77:6).

Sensing that the book contains great knowledge, John weeps that its contents are inaccessible. However, one of the twenty-four elders comforts John, telling him that Jesus Christ has the power to open the book. The twenty-four elders then sing out joyous praise to Him who opens the book, to the One who has power over each of the seals (each of the one-thousand-year periods) and all that are in them. Joining the chorus are myriads of God's creations worshiping the Lord and Savior Jesus Christ.

In Revelation 6, John witnesses Christ opening each seal, the first through the sixth. John sees the history of each thousand-year time period represented by different beasts. The sixth is marked by convulsions in the cosmos and reelings on the earth.

The stage is now ready for the opening of the seventh seal and for the *eschaton* (the end times, the last days). But we will not be reviewing here the many things that occur in the seventh seal—the plagues, destruction, wickedness, unleashing of Satan's power, the suffering and persecution of God's righteous Saints, the Restoration and preaching of the gospel message, and the eventual destruction of Babylon and her wickedness—all of which are detailed in Revelation 7–18.

Simply summarized, these twelve chapters fulfill the first two broad themes: (1) Satan attacks the work of God and the Saints of God, and (2) the suffering righteous endure through faith until the end.

REVELATION 19–20

These two chapters fulfill the third broad theme: the Lord comes triumphant to the destruction of the forces of evil and to the justification and sanctification of the Saints. When we arrive on the scene again in these chapters, we find the blessed righteous singing praises to the Lord.

In Revelation 19, the great invitation to the marriage supper of the Lamb goes forth. Only the righteous who have endured the crosses of the world, who have had faith in the Lamb of God, are invited to feast at table of their King and Groom. Consider that we are invited to the table/altar of the Great King every week in remembrance of His loving sacrifice. May this be but a weekly practice and preparation for that holy meal we desire to partake with Him when He returns?

At this point in the vision, John witnesses the glorious manifestation of the Lord Jesus Christ, arrayed in His kingly robes and descending from heaven to the marriage supper He has prepared. The wicked are then destroyed. In Revelation 20, the adversary is chained down to hell while the righteous dead are raised out of the pit of death in resurrection. They receive that most coveted promise that "on such the second death [spiritual death] hath no power, but they shall be priests of God and of Christ, and shall reign with him a thousand years" (Revelation 20:6). John then sees that at the end of the thousand years Satan will be loosed for short season, and some of the nations will be deceived and gathered again to battle against the people of God. John sees that ultimately God triumphs, and all of the resurrected dead stand before the Lord to be judged of their thoughts, words, and deeds according to those things recorded in the book of life.

REVELATION 21–22 AND CONCLUSION

The final two chapters of the book of Revelation follow the broad theme of final peace and joy of the righteous with God in the New Jerusalem on earth. At the end of the Millennium, after Satan has been ultimately disposed of and the wicked justly judged, John sees the holy city of the New Jerusalem descending from heaven. The righteous children of God are comforted from all that has hurt them, and the promise of eternal life is secured: "I am Alpha and Omega, the beginning and the end. I will give unto him that is athirst of the fountain of water of life freely. He that overcometh shall inherit all things; and I will be his God, and he shall be my son" (Revelation 21:6–7).

John's final vistas of the vision include a description of the New Jerusalem, a city built of the most precious elements—a place where darkness is never found and righteousness forever abounds. John also learns that the tree of life is at the center of the city for all the saved to freely partake; God himself will forever be in their midst before their faces.

What greater blessings of untold joy and harmony could any child of God ever desire? John closes his vision with the admonition and testimony that what he has seen is true, that the Lord Jesus Christ comes quickly, and that those who hearken to the words of his prophecy will find themselves inheriting the joys the eternal city of the New Jerusalem, worlds without end. Amen.

CONCLUSION

I hope that you have experienced joy and enlightenment to dig deeper into the context, history, symbolism, and meaning of select scriptural passages from the New Testament. This precious record from God witnesses of the love of God as shown through Jesus Christ. As we treasure the word of God by reading, by searching to understand His words, and most importantly, by diligently seeking to apply the principles of truths we discover, our lives will be filled with peace, our hearts will swell with gratitude, our love for God and our neighbors will be full, and we will experience the grand promise of scripture, "They lived after the manner of happiness" (2 Nephi 5:27).

ABOUT THE AUTHOR

TAYLOR HALVERSON IS A TEACHING and learning consultant at Brigham Young University; a member of the Book of Mormon Central executive committee; a columnist for the *Deseret News*; a founder of the BYU Creativity, Innovation, and Design group; a travel leader to Mesoamerica and the Holy Land; and the chief innovation officer at Vereo Training.

At BYU, Taylor has taught Book of Mormon, Old Testament, history of creativity, innovation boot camp, basic entrepreneurship skills, and an interdisciplinary design course called "Illuminating the Scriptures: Designing Innovative Study Tools."

Taylor received a BA in ancient Near Eastern studies from BYU, an MA in Biblical studies from Yale, an MS in instructional systems technology from Indiana University, a PhD in instructional systems technology from Indiana University, and a PhD in Judaism and Christianity in antiquity from Indiana University.

He has published and presented widely on scripture, technology, teaching, and learning. For more, check out taylorhalverson.com.